CIVIL-MILITARY RELATIONS IN TAIWAN

Identity and Transformation

CIVIL-MILITARY RELATIONS IN TAIWAN

Identity and Transformation

BY

DEAN KARALEKAS

Taiwan Center for Security Studies, Taiwan

United Kingdom — North America — Japan
India — Malaysia — China

Emerald Publishing Limited
Howard House, Wagon Lane, Bingley BD16 1WA, UK

First edition 2018

Reprints and permissions service
Contact: permissions@emeraldinsight.com

British Library Cataloguing in Publication Data
A catalogue record for this book is available from the British
Library

ISBN: 978-1-78756-482-4 (Print)
ISBN: 978-1-78756-479-4 (Online)
ISBN: 978-1-78756-481-7 (Epub)

Printed and bound by CPI Group (UK) Ltd, Croydon, CR0 4YY

ISOQAR certified
Management System,
awarded to Emerald
for adherence to
Environmental
standard
ISO 14001:2004.

ISOQAR
REGISTERED
Certificate Number 1985
ISO 14001

INVESTOR IN PEOPLE

CONTENTS

List of Figures   vii

List of Tables   ix

Introduction: The Armed Forces of the Republic of China (ROC)   1

1. Moskos's Postmodern Military Model   11

2. Ethnic Self-identification   41

3. Threat Perception in Taiwan   51

4. Force Structure and Conscientious Objectors   67

5. Major Mission Definition   83

6. Dominant Military Professional and Civilian Employees   93

7. Spouses and the Military Community   103

8. Women and the Military   111

9. Homosexuals in the ROC Military   129

10. Public Attitudes and Media Relations   135

11. Summary of Findings   151

12. Policy Recommendations   161

References   181

Index   195

LIST OF FIGURES

Chapter 3

Figure 3.1   Threat Perception.   59

Chapter 4

Figure 4.1   Preferred Conscription Policy.   74

Figure 4.2   Preferred Conscientious Objection Policy. .   78

Figure 4.3   Willingness to Allow Own Children to Enlist.   79

Figure 4.4   Willingness to Fight by Ethnic Self-
identification.   81

Chapter 6

Figure 6.1   Main Problem Facing the Military.   99

Chapter 8

Figure 8.1   Opinion on Opening Military Jobs to
Women.   126

Chapter 9

Figure 9.1   Policy on Homosexuals in the Military. . . .   134

Chapter 10

Figure 10.1   Faith in the Military's Ability to Defend
Taiwan.   141

Figure 10.2   Fairness and Impartiality of the Military. . .   144

Figure 10.3   Opinion on Media Coverage of the
Military.   150

LIST OF TABLES

Chapter 1

Table 1.1   Dimensions of the Postmodern Military
Model.   13

Chapter 3

Table 3.1   Cross-Strait Worry: One-By-One
Correlations.   61

Chapter 10

Table 10.1   Faith in the Military to Defend Taiwan,
by Ethnicity.   143

Chapter 11

Table 11.1   Descriptive Statistics.   152

Table 11.2   Summary: Taiwan and the Postmodern
Military Model.   155

INTRODUCTION: THE ARMED FORCES OF THE REPUBLIC OF CHINA (ROC)

The Armed Forces of the Republic of China (ROC) refers to the country's Army, Air Force, Navy, Marine Corps, and Military Police Force. Originally called the National Revolutionary Army at its inception in 1925 in China, it was renamed the Republic of China Armed Forces with the 1947 promulgation of the ROC Constitution. Since 1949, the force's primary goal was the ROC government's objective of retaking the mainland (China) from the Communists. Known as Project National Glory, this imperative was front-and-center until the 1970s. As the military balance in the Taiwan Strait began to shift from one favoring the ROC to one favoring the People's Republic of China (PRC), the focus of the ROC military began to shift to a defensive posture, defending the islands of Penghu, Quemoy, Matsu, and Taiwan (Formosa) from invasion by China's People's Liberation

Army (PLA). The PLA remains the predominant — indeed, the only — threat to the ROC today.

While still the National Revolutionary Army, it was essentially the military arm of the Kuomintang (KMT). Even after becoming the ROC Armed Forces in 1947, and relocating to Taiwan in 1949, the ROC remained a de-facto one-party state ruled by the KMT, and the military remained essentially the KMT Army, with political indoctrination to ensure the loyalty of its members, and political officers and commissioners installed in each company's unit to monitor that loyalty.[1] Today, the political warfare department does not wield the power it once did, and political officers can no longer take over command of the unit in the name of ensuring loyalty to the government as they once could.

As a result of this history, the military has long been regarded by most Minnan-speaking Taiwanese (those whose ancestors moved to the island starting in the seventeenth century, as opposed to the so-called Mainlanders who arrived from mainland China following the 1949 KMT defeat at the hands of the Communists) as being very much the "KMT army." The extent to which this perception persists is very much of interest when determining the civil—military relationship in Taiwan. Also because of this history, however, the ROC military has had far fewer of the problems associated with military interventions in politics, as has historically been the case in such democratized Asian states as Indonesia, Thailand, South Korea, and Japan. Unlike these nations, there has never been an attempted military coup d'état in the ROC on Taiwan — a testament to the Chiang regime's grip on power and the tight control it exerted over its military. Thus, on the one hand, conditions exist today for low popular regard for the military, especially as regards a military career, and yet the principle of civilian control over the military — a doctrine in military and political science — is perhaps stronger in Taiwan than in many comparable Asian states.

In the 1970s, when first the United Nations, and later the United States, derecognized the ROC in favor of the PRC, the leadership in Taipei deemed – correctly – that anti-Communism would no longer be as strong a force for cementing alliances with the West as it had been up to that point, and so Chiang Ching-kuo began slowly to loosen the reins of the dictatorship which had theretofore been largely successful in repelling domestic calls for social liberalization and eventually democracy. In 1987, the 38 long years of Martial Law came to an end, and with it the White Terror period. Thus, Taiwan became one of the nations that threw off the shackles of authoritarianism in the Third Wave of democratization that swept the globe.

This democratization, along with the nation's impressive economic growth – known as the Taiwan Miracle – served to create the conditions wherein rapid changes to the social structure and society's values would take place. In the wake of the lifting of Martial Law, Taiwan saw enormous changes in almost all respects, including the growth of a civil society, the widespread acceptance of Western liberal values, a thriving political environment wherein leaders vie for votes to represent their constituencies, and most recently, a deep belief among young people in social justice to the point where they are willing to take to the streets to protest unconstitutional actions on the part of government representatives (Blundell, 2012). Compared to the social landscape just three decades ago, it is a completely different Taiwan.

Yet despite these fundamental changes, the security situation across the Taiwan Strait remains tense. The PRC is still intent on annexing Taiwan and has yet to renounce the use of force as a means to that end. An estimated 1,600 missiles of the PLA Rocket Force (formerly the Second Artillery

Corps) stand arrayed along China's southern coast, targeted squarely on Taiwan. The faceoff across the strait is a product of the Cold War international order, and while the Cold War itself has long since ended, the situation in the Taiwan Strait remains very much the same, with the threat from China ever-present.

The weapons used by Beijing to coerce Taipei into rapprochement have changed as China's economic and military might have grown in recent decades. Whereas once, the PLA was essentially a large, technically unsophisticated standing army geared toward defense of China's vast territory and the subjugation of its peoples, the PRC's rapid economic growth has enabled the purchase (and theft through espionage) of advanced weapons systems and technologies which have seen the PLA become a high-tech fighting force, and the PLA Navy (PLAN) shift its focus on coastal defense to adopt not-so-far-fetched ambitions of one day fielding a blue-water navy.

Moreover, following the doctrine of Unrestricted Warfare first enunciated by PLA colonels Qiao Liang and Wang Xiangsui, China has succeeded in creating the conditions whereby its economic and supply-chain integration with the economy of Taiwan can be used as a weapon to coerce capitulation. In addition to the economic sphere, Chinese attempts to effect rapprochement on Beijing's terms take the form of manipulation in a number of fields, including ethnocultural (promoting the idea that the Taiwanese people are descendants of Yan and Yellow Emperor), sophisticated electronics (PLA hackers are constantly launching cyberattacks on the Taiwan government and corporate websites and servers, often as a means to test out new techniques before using them on targets in the United States), and covert espionage (Chinese intelligence operatives have managed to turn many current and former military members, as well as civilians), among others.

Moreover, the situation has become increasingly complicated as the ROC military's erstwhile patron, the KMT, which was once seen as the anti-Communist party, has in recent years become the party most committed to eventual unification with Communist China. From 2008 to 2016, under a KMT administration, the door has been opened to thousands of Chinese tourists visiting Taiwan, direct flights have begun plying the airways between the two countries, and several trade deals have been signed.[2]

So there exists a situation in which Taiwan society has moved forward, both economically as well as politically, from dictatorship, through democratization, and into a truly open and free society dedicated to fairness and equality, and yet the security situation remains unchanged, with the threat of invasion ever-present. As a result, the military tasked with confronting this threat has remained one of the largest social organs on the island resistant to change. Much has been made of the military culture in the ROC armed forces, how it is risk-averse and resistant to change. Yet change it must, if it is truly going to represent — as well as once again play an integral part in — the society it defends. ROC leaders understand that such change is necessary, and in an effort to remake the military into a social institution more in line with modern Taiwan society, an effort was launched in 2008 to transition to an All-Volunteer Force (AVF). Unfortunately, this effort failed, and during the eight years of the President Ma Ying-Jeou administration, recruitment targets and deadlines for completion have consistently gone unmet (McCauley, 2016, p. 6). This volume argues that, while the AVF transition is the wrong goal, the instinct for change and modernization is essentially correct. Thus the challenge faced by Taiwan's leaders is to establish a blueprint for a rebranded ROC military that continues to form a credible defense against China yet reflects the modern-day realities of contemporary Taiwan. In order to solve this problem, an assessment first must be made of the current state of the ROC military. Fortunately, military sociologists have developed tools for just such an assessment.

THE POSTMODERN MILITARY MODEL

The postmodern military model (PMMM) identifies three distinct stages in military transformation: the modern stage, the late modern stage, and the postmodern stage. Within this approach, each stage is described and identified using 11 dimensions (see Table 1). In the dimension of threat perception, for example, a modern (pre-Cold War/1900—1945) military faces the threat of invasion by the standing army of an enemy state. A late modern (Cold War/1945—1990) military faces the threat of nuclear war. A postmodern (post-Cold War/since 1990) military faces challenges such as terrorism, ethnic conflict, and other sub-national threats. In each of the 11 dimensions, the military of each stage is measurably different from the previous stage.

Very often in Taiwan, when a new government initiative or institutional body needs to be created, there is a tendency to look abroad for a template that can be applied. Due to its close historical relationship to Taiwan, especially during the post-war era, the United States often serves as the source of that template, such as the ROC National Communications Commission.[3] While this example is a relatively successful example of such transplantation, others have not fared so well. Moreover, the situation regarding the military is quite different. It has been suggested that the American experience of ending conscription in the early 1970s was the model, or at least the inspiration, for President Ma's desire to do the same in Taiwan. While the concluding chapter goes into more detail as to why this is a mistaken assessment, suffice it to say here that the differences between the conditions of the two militaries are sufficiently wide that the one serves as a poor example for the other. The PMMM is an ideal tool with which to measure those differences and hence demonstrate the lack of applicability of the US example. As this research shows, there are significant differences in culture, circumstances, geopolitical currents, and other divergent factors that show the American example to be one that is not directly applicable to implementation in Taiwan.

Having said that, *the time is also ripe for a change*. Yet, the ROC military brass does not necessarily share this view. Indeed, one of the criticisms that has been levied against ROC military leaders is that they are highly cautious, conservative, and risk-averse (Tucker, 2005, p. 157). Nevertheless, change there must be, as a recent case involving the death of a conscript due to harsh punishment at the hands of his superior officers demonstrates. One must ask the question, what is the place of the military in Taiwan society? That is an essential question that this book will endeavor to clarify.

In order to understand the place of the ROC military in Taiwan society, this research was aimed at studying the impact of self-identification on a variety of perceptions of the ROC military, and to what degree the beliefs of Taiwan citizens about the ROC armed forces are colored by the way they identify ethnically, as either Chinese or Taiwanese (中國人 or 台灣人). The question of identity, and the various ways that are expressed, is central to any understanding of Taiwan society, and thus aspects of identity such as ethnic self-identification, as well as the associated issues of political party identification and vision of the future of Taiwan (especially as regards the independence vs unification issue), are of paramount importance in any discussion of Taiwan society. They are therefore of no less importance in determining the state of civil—military relations in the country.

Ultimately, this volume is intended to provide policy-makers within the ROC government and military with an understanding of the current military—society relationship, so that they may proceed with their efforts to create a more accountable military. This is an especially urgent problem given the ROC government's policy goal of shifting to a professional military. Should that goal be pursued to completion, then the task of enticing the nation's best and brightest high-school graduates to choose a career in the armed forces will become all the more difficult, especially if the current low levels of morale continue to exist in the ranks. Before policy-makers and officers can expect to be able to address the AVF issue, they need to understand the root causes of the schism that exists between military and society. The practical outcomes of research such as this will be important in that endeavor. Moreover, the outcomes of this research may also help theorists gain a better understanding of the dynamics of the famously elusive Taiwan identity.

This study is designed to have direct practical value to ROC military officers and government policymakers, especially those charged with charting the ideological course of the ROC armed forces. As it stands now, troop morale is low, and the public distrusts the neutrality of the armed forces (Swaine & Mulvenon, 2001, p. 75). The training regimen and prevalent ideology within the army may be a contributor to this phenomenon, as it potentially clashes with the ethnic loyalties of its members. Changing the ideological imprint of a large organization is a difficult prospect at best, and at worst an impossible undertaking. Moreover, the plan suffers from a lack of public interest, exacerbated by memories of the island's militarized past, which conspire to stand in the way of effective military reform and development (Setzekorn, 2014).

However, if sufficient political capital can be harnessed — building upon initial efforts to transfer over to a professional military — then it may provide a unique opportunity to implement scientifically valid processes, right at the beginning, thus laying a foundation upon which the new military structure can build a healthy, effective fighting force that is in lockstep with the society it protects. Now is the time to undertake a thorough examination of conditions in the ROC military and society, determine the best course of action, and follow it.

In addition to being of direct practical value, this book offers theoretical and conceptual contributions as well. Understanding the link between ethnic identification and perceptions of a large social institution such as the military has value beyond just a military setting, as well as in countries other than Taiwan. The dynamics in play are not unlike those in several other countries around the world: specifically, ethnic identification in a nonhomogeneous society. Moreover, the study's conclusions include the observation that while Taiwan's military scores in the higher level in some of the PMMM dimensions, it scores in the lower level in many others. Far from disqualifying the model as an analytical tool, it enhances its usefulness. The way the model has been employed to measure Taiwan's military—society relationship may be used in other countries as well that do not themselves follow the Western pattern of development, but rather may be closer to what Taiwan has experienced.

NOTES

1. This practice was employed initially by Chiang Kai-shek and Chiang Ching-kuo as a means of ensuring loyalty to the KMT at a

time when Communist agents and sympathizers routinely infiltrated the ranks of the armed forces, and entire frontline units have been known to have defected to the PRC.

2. These include the controversial Cross-Strait Agreement on Trade in Services and the Economic Cooperation Framework Agreement (ECFA), which has led to a drop in trade and a slide in Taiwan's trade surplus with China (Turton, 2016b).

3. The ROC National Communications Commission was formed in 2006, and was directly patterned on the US Federal Communications Commission.

CHAPTER 1

MOSKOS'S POSTMODERN MILITARY MODEL

The postmodern military model (PMMM), promulgated by Moskos, Williams, and Segal (2000), posits that militaries faced with a shift from the threat perception of war (such as enemy invasion or nuclear attack) to primarily nontraditional threats (such as terrorism and ethnic violence) undergo changes to their force structure, personnel requirements, and their relationship to the wider society. This work is built upon the foundation established by Morris Janowitz, who in *Professional Soldier: A Social and Political Portrait* (1960) famously used the techniques of social science to examine the relationship between the military establishment and civil society in the United States. Janowitz first commented on trends such as the trend toward a managerial-type officer and increasing civilianization that Moskos would build upon and include in the PMMM.

The model was originally developed as a means of examining the changes taking place in the US military by establishing a framework for military transformation, from the mass standing army dedicated to warfighting that was marked by a different ethos than the civilian society which it was charged with protecting, to a more multipurpose force marked by the professional soldier, more civilian interpenetration, and responding to a very different threat profile. The PMMM has been employed not just to describe conditions in America, but as a means of studying the shifts that have been experienced by a number of militaries in various countries. An example is the shift that occurred in the western nations in the post-Cold War era, becoming what Moskos et al. (2000) term "postmodern" militaries. Many militaries have undergone such a shift, primarily those of the western European and North American nations, as they and their associated societies transitioned into the postmodern era. Thus, in addition to being used as a descriptive tool to describe military transformation in these countries, the model may also be applicable as a predictive tool to assess the state of civil—military relations in these and other countries. Moskos is one of the world's foremost military sociologists and his theories have been essential in our understanding of civil—military relations, and so it is important for planners and policy-makers in Taiwan to take such scholarship into account as they see their society evolving toward postmodernism and attempt to push their military to follow. The effort to transition to an all-volunteer force is, in essence, an attempt to follow a western pattern of development, but one that has been embarked upon without appropriate research, and so it stands to reason that the very model that describes this pattern so well be used to assess the Republic of China (ROC) military's readiness for such a change.

In determining how the ROC military fits into the definition of a modern, late modern, or postmodern military according to the theoretical construct developed by Moskos et al. (2000), an assessment must be made of the 11 distinct dimensions of the model (see **Table 1.1**). The model has been applied to a study of the ROC military before, in a study by Chia-sheng Chen (2009), who used it as a framework to explain the organizational changes witnessed by the ROC military since 1949 and illustrate how this transformation was associated with Taiwan's democratization, economic growth, and foreign military assistance. Chen concluded that the ROC military exhibited the characteristics of a late

Table 1.1. Dimensions of the Postmodern Military Model.

Dimension	Modern (1900–1945)	Late Modern (1945–1990)	Postmodern (1990–present)
Threat perception	Enemy invasion	Nuclear war	Subnational
Force structure	Mass army (conscription)	Large professional	Small professional
Mission definition	Homeland defense	Alliance support	MOOTW
Mil. professional	Combat leader	Manager/ Technician	Soldier–statesman/ Scholar
Public attitude	Supportive	Ambivalent	Indifferent
Media relations	Incorporated	Manipulated	Courted
Civilian employees	Minor	Medium	Major
Women's role	Excluded or separate	Partial integration	Full integration
Spouses	Integral	Partial involvement	Removed
Homosexuals	Punished	Discharged	Accepted
Conscientious objection	Limited	Permitted	Civilian service

modern military. In detailing the transformation of the
ROC military, Chen identified four discrete stages of
Taiwan's political-military development. First is the joint
defense stage (1949–1978), dominated by the US–Taiwan
mutual defense treaty. Following this, the self-defense stage
(1979–1986) saw a shift of responsibility for Taiwan's
defense falling squarely on the ROC's shoulders, with little
to no assistance from the international community. Next is
the democratization stage (1987–1996), marked by changes
in military organization in response to wider social shifts.
Finally, the democracy stage (1997 to present) saw a series
of changes to ROC military culture and organization, influenced by the transfer of political power in 2000 and other
democratic and social forces. These distinct stages, or eras,
are a useful hermeneutic tool and will be referenced in this
study.

1.1. PMMM DIMENSIONS

There are several dimensions for which public perception is
extremely helpful in making a determination as to their
place on the PMMM spectrum. Moreover, most assessments that have come before do not incorporate survey
data on public attitudes but rather based their assessments
on other measures – such as military members' attitudes,
for example, or an analysis of laws and regulations. This
approach, while adequate, can only benefit from incorporation of public perceptions, and this is the best way
to develop an appreciation for the state of civil–military
relations. Let us first review the spectrum of the PMMM
dimensions.

1.1.1. Perceived Threat

The relationship between a nation's military and the wider society is greatly influenced by the perceived threat. Not only does the threat of war — from what likely enemy or enemies, what sort of war, how imminent is the threat, and other similar factors defining the said threat — contribute greatly to the structure and operation of the military tasked to defend against it, but also it is ever-present in the minds of the nation's civilian population as well. As such, it is a defining factor in society—military relations, and the first listed by Moskos et al. (2000) in enunciating the PMMM.

In the modern military — that which existed primarily in the pre-Cold War period, from roughly 1900 to the end of the Second World War in 1945 — the threat that was most commonly perceived was an invasion. Indeed, since man first raised sticks and rocks to take that which was his neighbor's, the threat of invasion of one's territory (or later, that of a political ally) has been the main concern of statesmen and military commanders seeking strategies for defense. Naturally, this necessitated (both for the defenders as well as the aggressors) large standing armies for much of this period, influenced as time progressed by advances in weaponry and tactics. Societies, still largely agrarian, lived in constant proximity to the threat of foreign armies marching in, with the risk that their farmland would become battlefields.

This calculus changed greatly in the Cold War as the nature of the perceived threat evolved from one of invasion to the specter of nuclear war. The early twentieth century witnessed mankind's great technological leaps forward and advances in industrial-scale production turned to the practice of war, making it possible for the old paradigm of armed invasion to be conducted on a scale never before imagined, in terms not only of speed and efficiency, but also of body count. Not only did the savagery of the Great War, and after it the Second World War, usher in new aspirations for nationhood (in the form of the European Union and other transnational regional groupings predicated on a new conception of the value of national sovereignty), but they also spurred scientific and technological developments in the manufacture of weapons that would change the threat perception of nations forever: they led to the development of nuclear weapons.

At first, atomic weapons were little more than a terrifyingly effective bomb, with admittedly previously unseen side effects in the form of radiation and fallout. Once both sides in the bipolar world order that coalesced after World War II (WWII) had acquired not only the weapons but also systems capable of delivering them to enemy territory across great distances, the primary threat to nations, their militaries, and their societies became that of a nuclear attack. Peace — or at the very least, the absence of open hostilities — during this era was predicated on a precarious balance perhaps best described by the concept of mutually assured destruction (MAD); nuclear weapons are so deadly and so terrifying, and there are so many of them ready for deployment against the United States and her allies as well as against the Union of Soviet Socialist Republics, that any first strike would be quickly followed by a conflagration capable of effectively destroying both sides. Societies on either side of the iron curtain were acutely aware of the deadly potentialities of nuclear war — made so by their respective governments not only as a means to ensure that protective measures could be performed, but also more importantly as a means of building nationalist-based support for the political and military regime, and against the much-feared enemy. This dynamic defined perceived threat during the late modern military, lasting from roughly 1945 to 1990.

This tenuous balance, predicated on MAD, saw the world survive to the end of the Cold War, after the dissolution of the Soviet Union and the fall of the Berlin Wall. After a short period during which the western nations enjoyed a peace dividend marked by lower defense spending and the spread of democratic institutions abroad with an almost missionary zeal, a new threat perception emerged, and one that was so terrifying and chaotic that many longed for the simpler days of the Cold War threat of nuclear annihilation. This new and current threat perception is, of course, terrorism. This, along with other subnational threats, was largely poorly perceived by society in general until the attacks on September 11, 2001. As much as the Japanese attack on Pearl Harbor in 1941, this event was a game changer in terms of threat perception by Americans, and to a lesser degree by nations around the globe.

In addition to terrorism, other aspects of subnational threats include ethnic conflicts, such as the Balkanization of the former Yugoslavia early in the postmodern era, or the attempted genocides and ethnic cleansing perpetrated on ethnic groups in Rwanda, for example, and the Central African Republic, giving lie to the international community's post-WWII vow of "never again."

No longer is the threat of nuclear annihilation society's boogeyman, unless it pertains to the possible use of a dirty bomb by an otherwise technologically unsophisticated terrorist group such as Al-Qaeda or the Islamic State, or one of the domestic so-called lone-wolf terrorists inspired and sometimes supported by these groups. Moreover, with threat perception dominated by terrorism, it takes the impetus for the buildup to a war out of the hands of high politics and delivers it into the hands of jihadists and — as perceived by citizens in the West — madmen. War no longer is primarily an extension of politics, to paraphrase von Clausewitz, but the whim of a madman. Thus, the lack of any guiding logic behind the decision to wage war creates an even deeper sense of loss of control on the part of the citizen, and an ever-greater respect for the soldier to put himself in harm's way in a war in which the other side is not bound by the Geneva Conventions and which famously takes no prisoners, unless it is for a subsequent videotaped beheading.

1.1.2. Force Structure

Up to and during the modern era (1900–1945), the ROC military has followed the model described by Moskos et al. and concerned itself mainly with fronting a large standing army. Even such conscript armies, it should be noted, rely on a core group of professional soldiers in the officer class, but most importantly in the class of non-commissioned officers (usually sergeants and above) to provide guidance, cohesion, and stability. Moreover, even conscript armies require some professional soldiers in certain trades that require technical proficiency.

During the Cold War, late modern (1945–1990) militaries generally shifted their force structure somewhat – armed forces were still large in terms of troop numbers, but they were increasingly professional. With the shift in threat perception from invasion to nuclear attack, and with the advancements made in weapons systems and military strategy during and after WWII, nations required more from their soldiers than simply being proficient with a gun. During this period, many nations made the shift to an All-Volunteer Force (AVF), recruiting a higher-caliber, better-motivated serviceman, especially in trades that required technical sophistication.

By the postmodern era (1990–present), most of those nations that had managed to avoid making the AVF transition found it amenable to do so, with the end of the Cold War and a redefinition of the threat perception. The new threat of subnational, largely ethnic-based, violence and the rise of Islamic terrorism demanded a new force structure. The requirement for professionalism in the armed services was even more pronounced. To engage in peacekeeping deployments under the UN umbrella, and to fight jihadists in the deserts of Iraq and Afghanistan, what was needed were greater numbers of the very type of special-forces soldiers that were the exception rather than the rule during the Cold War. The postmodern soldier is often deployed on missions requiring his interaction with people of different cultures and values, who speak another language and may be embroiled in a struggle involving religious or ethnic conflicts. This requires not only a higher standard in recruitment, but also a higher level of training in order to handle such challenges (Costa & Ivenicki, 2016, p. 226).

1.1.3. Major Mission Definition

The major mission definition is a critical aspect of any deter-mination of whether a particular nation's military has reached the postmodern stage. As a reflection of, and reaction to, the perceived threat, as well as a major contributing factor in decisions related to force structure, a military's main mis-sion definition is intrinsically tied in with the military's sense of itself, and therefore with its place in the larger society.

In the modern era (roughly 1900−1945) − and indeed, for much of history leading up to that era − the major mis-sion definition of a military was one of homeland defense. This reflects the threat being primarily one of invasion and the force structure being a large standing army fed by conscription. In the late modern (Cold War/1945−1990) military, the major mission definition changed to reflect the realities of that age, and became one of alliance support. As described by Moskos et al., the postmodern (post-Cold War/since 1990) military is marked by a subsequent shift from a mission definition based on alliance support to one based on a host of new types of mission theretofore largely unseen. These include peacekeeping operations, international Humanitarian Assistance and Disaster Relief (HA/DR), and other non-combat taskings grouped under the category of Military Operations Other Than War (MOOTW).

1.1.4. Dominant Military Professional

The postmodern military is marked by shifts in perceived threat, from one predicated on nuclear attack to a host of threats at the subnational level including terrorist attacks and ethnic violence. This naturally necessitates a reevaluation of the major mission definition and hence a redrawing of the nation's force structure in order to accomplish that mission. The dominant military professional will likewise undergo a shift in order to exercise the most effective leadership in the new military/threat environment. Moskos et al. identified how the focus of the dominant military professional changed from the modern (pre-Cold War/1900–1945) period from one of a combat leader proficient in the art of war and in exercising effective leadership under combat conditions, to a more managerial role in the late modern (Cold War/1945–1990) military, and thence to a skill set heavy on diplomacy and scholarship in the postmodern (post-Cold War/since 1990) era.

It is self-evident that, for much of human history, the best military leaders have been those most capable of fighting and winning wars, with little focus on – indeed, with little need for – the skills of the technician or the diplomat. From Publius Cornelius Scipio Africanus to Vice Admiral Horatio Lord Nelson, and from Xiang Yu to Sun Tzu, military leaders of the premodern period were renowned for their leadership, tactics, and warfighting prowess, and earned promotion and glory on that basis. This continued into the modern period, coming to an end only with the Cold War. This new threat, and hence the new means of fighting it, demanded new skills: relatively few conventional wars were waged compared to the previous eras, at least by the global superpowers holding large stockpiles of nuclear weapons, and so as a means of earning promotion, glory on the battlefield gave way to technological and administrative proficiency, befitting the new era of technological weaponry that had become the decisive factor in defeating the enemy. This shift is perhaps best described by Janowitz (1960). In the postmodern military, the skills that lead to success and promotion, as identified by Moskos et al., are those of the soldier–scholar and the soldier–statesman. This is especially important in the realm of civil–military relations, where military leaders must handle such challenges as dealing with a free and independent media, or navigating the intricacies of international relations.

1.1.5. Public Attitude Toward the Military

At the very heart of the issue of civil–military relations, and the focus of this study, is the public's attitude toward the military. Regardless of whether there is civilian leadership of the armed forces, or a significant public-relations effort being made to humanize the army and those serving in it, the bottom line comes back to just how the members of the public perceive the military, and what are their feelings toward it. This is an important variable in the work of

Moskos et al., as they sought to examine and define the post-modern military concept, and it is arguably one over which military and political leaders have the least control. Indeed, it is the sum and the result of the other factors combined, and hence one that requires close study.

As a nation's military shifts from the modern to the late modern, and thence to the postmodern, the national public's attitude toward the military likewise changes. In the modern (pre-Cold War/1900—1945) military, the public is supportive of the military. The dominant perceived threat — one of enemy invasion — is felt keenly by the population at large, and hence there is often a sense of admiration and respect for those warriors who put themselves in harm's way to protect the nation. Moreover, there is often a policy of universal conscription in effect during this phase, and therefore a greater portion of the population familiar — and therefore sympathetic — with the realities of military life and service.

By the late modern (Cold War/1945—1990) period, the public becomes more ambivalent about the military. Support remains, but it is not as strong, with anti-military sentiments appearing in some parts of society, such as academia and among the intelligentsia. By the postmodern (post-Cold War/ since 1990) era, the public attitude toward the military is largely one of indifference. By this phase, many western nations had completed their transition to the all-volunteer force, and the military life is distinct and separate from society at large, with the realities of that lifestyle largely alien to much of the population. This lack of familiarity helps create a gulf between military and society, with much less overlap than in previous generations.

A good indicator of how the public views the military can be seen in portrayals of military personnel in popular media. During the modern era and immediately afterward, military personnel are largely treated as heroes in movies and television programs: though not exclusively so, this was a trend. American movies — especially science-fiction movies — of the 1950s and early 1960s largely treated soldiers as the saviors and problem solvers while depicting scientists as, if not the antagonists, the inadvertent catalysts for death and destruction through the technology that they unleash. High-profile examples include The Thing from Another World (1951) and the superb Forbidden Planet (1956). These and like films met the public's desire to see ordinary people, and in many cases ordinary soldiers (much as their sons, fathers, and brothers had been in WWII), defeat the figure of the mad scientist — itself a caricature that fed into the public's distrust of intellectuals and scientists who had been responsible for unleashing, respectively, Communism and nuclear bombs upon the world. Moreover, the monsters in many films of the era were the explicit byproduct of nuclear radiation, most famously in the form of the immensely popular Godzilla movies. Much has been written about the famous movie monster, popularly as a reflection of Japan's anxiety about the destructiveness of nuclear technology.

It is interesting to note that as the modern military model gave way to the late modern, the dominant military professional shifted from one of combat leader to technician; this shift is evident in popular media, especially in films that portray the military in a generally positive light. The 1986 film Top Gun, for example, had as its heroes pilots, or naval aviators, as opposed to the platoon commander or junior officer. Unlike Top Gun, which received support from the US Navy in exchange for input in how the Navy was depicted, most American films of the era were critical of the military, a reflection of the American public's lingering shame over both the conduct of the war in Vietnam and how its veterans were treated upon their return.

By the postmodern period, the depiction of military personnel has largely degenerated into, as Moskos terms it, buffoonish characters, and in many cases outright antagonists. Moskos mentions Broken Arrow (1996) and The Rock (1996) as famous examples of popular films in which military officers act, essentially, like terrorists. In both cases, it is the lone hero who saves the day. Today, it is rare that a film with a military component is made in which the military itself, or the government, is not the antagonist. A good illustration of this shift is in the big-screen franchise that is an adaptation of the *Mission: Impossible* television series from the 1960s and early 1970s. In that program, the heroes are government agents (though never explicitly stated, likely CIA) who use sleight of hand, elaborate deception, and grifting techniques to advance America's interests in the world (and at home) by foiling the plots of Communist regimes, South American dictatorships, and organized crime syndicates. The assignments, famously delivered clandestinely via tiny, self-destructing tapes hidden around Los Angeles, were never questioned, nor were the rightness of the heroes' actions. In contrast, the big-budget films produced by and starring Tom Cruise almost uniformly have members of the same government organization for which the heroes work as their villains. The Bourne films — adaptations of the Robert Ludlum series — are no different, with the CIA being the ultimate baddies. Indeed, one would be hard-pressed to find a military-themed movie made by Hollywood that isn't either critical of the military as an institution or having the villain somewhere higher up in the chain of command. Otherwise, such films would be deemed overly jingoistic and therefore anathema to the sensibilities of much of the nation's media elites.

1.1.6. Media Relations

The news media can be viewed as the communal space through which members of a society interact: it provides the population with a window on the world, and a recounting — and increasingly, analysis — of events taking place within the nation itself. This continues to be true even in the Internet age, especially if one considers social media (as well as bloggers and other nontraditional news sources) as a mere technological advance of the same social institution. Thus, the media's relationship with and position toward the military is an extremely important factor in assessing a nation's civil–military relations. Due to forces of change within the military, as well as within the media organizations themselves, this relationship has undergone a radical shift in the past century.

The modern (pre-Cold War/1900–1945) military enjoyed a cordial relationship with the media: they collaborated to achieve the same goals much of the time. Moskos et al. describe how the American media was essentially incorporated into the US military: citing the need for operational security, the military would routinely censor news reports, and for its part, the media accepted this state of affairs, with members of the press corps being commissioned military members and sometimes wearing uniforms. This was a time before the advent of globalization and the type of multinational media corporations that are the norm today: a country's media, while interested in selling papers and raising their revenue and profile, were likewise dedicated to assisting their home nation in conflicts such as the first and second world wars. This essentially put them on the same team as the military.

By the advent of the late modern (Cold War/1945–1990) military, many changes were being experienced by both institutions. The threat, force structure, and public perception of the military was changing during this period, but likewise the media was undergoing changes, most notably in terms of technology, with the advent of television and, specifically, the TV news program, which began to supplant the print media and radio as the conduit through which large swathes of the population derived its information. After the allied victory against Fascism in WWII, and in the ensuing fight against Communism that defined this era, the role of the Fourth Estate in a proper functioning democracy made it inappropriate for the press to be so incorporated into government, especially the armed forces. An increasing degree of media independence meant that the military could no longer outright control the press; nevertheless, it continued to manipulate the media, with such manipulation coming in the form of press pools, for example, groups of reporters and editors who had been vetted and approved by the government and who were granted access to military installations and personnel. While there was no actual censorship – at least not to the degree it was practiced during the modern era – the military did continue to influence media reports by choosing to whom it would grant access, and using such access as both a carrot and a stick.

Moreover, it was during this period that the press, armed with the powerful tool of visual imagery beamed right into the homes of the population, began to see its role less as one of supporting government efforts and more as a watchdog on government malfeasance. This was the era of the Watergate scandal, for example, as well as the ending of the McCarthyist witch-hunts largely at the hands of journalists like Edward R. Murrow. Given the new, almost opposing roles played in society by the military and the press, it was inevitable that the cozy relationship that they enjoyed during the modern era began unraveling during the late modern era. In the American context, perhaps the best illustration of this is in the coverage of the Vietnam War. For the first time, American families could see the battles that were taking place and put faces to the names on the casualty lists released by the Pentagon. In no small way, television contributed to the popular backlash against that war, and a subsequent redefinition of civil—military relations in the United States.

By the end of the Cold War, the postmodern (post-Cold War/since 1990) military had a relationship with the media that was very different indeed from what it had been in WWII. While the use of press pools continues, and there are continued attempts at manipulation and coercion of the media by the government such as that during the late modern period, the growth of the media industry has radically changed the press' susceptibility to such tactics. For one thing, media groups such as Fox News and CNN are no longer American media outlets, but global, with such regional operations as Fox News Asia and CNN International. Moreover, with huge assets at their disposal and the benefit of worldwide business and logistical networks, the media is not only no longer reliant on the military for access, but it also leads the way. As Moskos points out, reporters often arrive in a conflict zone prior to the troops deployed there, setting up operations and preparing to beam back unfiltered — at least, unfiltered by the US military — reports and images from the location immediately and independently via satellite. Indeed, it can be said that the situation vis-à-vis the media/military relationship has reversed, with the military courting assistance from a media that is increasingly powerful, independent, and (except in the case of the print media) flush with funds.

1.1.7. Civilian Employees

The changing face of a military as it moves into the postmodern phase is characterized in part by a blurring of the lines between civilian and service member. During the modern (pre-Cold War/1900—1945) era, civilians were a minor component of the armed forces in the West. It should be noted, however, that during the war effort, the process for conferring a commission was far less time-consuming and fraught with regulations than it is today, and many civilians whose skills were deemed useful were inducted into the Army, thus becoming serving military members while doing jobs that, in later eras, they would perform while still civilians, making the distinction largely an administrative one. For example, civilian airplane crews working for TWA and other airlines were granted military commissions, largely so that in case of capture, they would receive better treatment as prisoners of war under the Geneva Convention, being higher ranked than the level of sergeant.

Moreover, according to Faubion Bowers, who served as personal interpreter for Gen. Douglas MacArthur, any American who went to Washington and could pronounce "*Ohayo gozaimas*," (Good morning) or said they had been to Japan as a missionary's son or businessman or whatnot, was immediately given a commission in Military Intelligence (Bowers, n.d.). Commissions were given out so freely that, even in Hollywood, the heads of the major studios were made serving officers for helping the war effort through the production of patriotic films. Jack Warner, for example, was made a lieutenant colonel in the Army.

By war's end, and as the military entered the late modern (Cold War/1945—1990) phase, the use of civilian employees — especially those who remained civilians — had increased somewhat, with the civilian workforce being a medium component of the armed forces. Much of this came in the form of technical experts, especially in the Navy and Air Force, who had the specialized training to conduct repairs and maintenance on the increasingly high-tech weapons systems that were being developed during this era. As the threat perception shifted from fear of invasion to fear of nuclear attack, the technology and hence expertise required to deal with it shifted from a large standing army of men who could shoot a rifle to the kind of specialized skills that included proficiency with the latest technology. While much of these jobs could be performed by those in uniform, many more required specialized expertise that went beyond what the military could teach.

In addition to the high-tech positions that were increasingly being filled by civilians in this era, there were a number of low-tech or menial jobs that likewise were contracted out. As militaries made the AVF transition, recruiters understandably found it difficult to enlist personnel to perform such tasks as cleaning and painting rocks, much of which is derided as make-work. This is especially true of an institutional military, as opposed to an occupational one, wherein the nation's youth would seek an exciting, challenging career with opportunities for adventure and distinction, and not to perform menial, repetitive tasks. Moreover, contracting out such low-tech work to civilian employees is not only more cost-effective, but it also allows more time for recruits to receive more and better training, thus improving their overall operational skill set.

This trend of increasing civilian participation in the military continues into the postmodern (post-Cold War/since 1990) military, with most of the logistics and housekeeping duties required of overseas deployments being contracted to civilians during much of the 1990s, such as the US missions to Rwanda, Somalia, and Haiti. By the time of the US wars in Afghanistan and Iraq, not only were the aforementioned support services being conducted by civilians, but also the increasingly operational and combat roles as well. Politically, the US government wanted to draw down, or at least stem any increase of, military deployments to the Middle East, and yet operationally, more boots on the ground were required. Thus resulted the rapid rise of the civilian contractor. Private military companies such as Titan Corp., Aegis Defense Services, and most famously Blackwater USA began performing security and escort duties traditionally the purview of combat soldiers on a scale never before seen. Although the tradition of hiring mercenaries goes back millennia, the concept of the modern private military firm dates back to the mid-1960s, when the founder of the British Special Air Service (SAS) regiment, Sir David Stirling, co-founded WatchGuard International. In the early days of the postmodern military era, there were approximately fifty armed forces personnel for every contractor: by 2007, that number was 10 to 1 (Singer, 2007, p. 277).

1.1.8. Women's Role in the Military

The degree, as well as the nature, of participation by women is a marker not only of a military's transition to the postmodern model, but also that of society in general. As western societies moved into the postmodern age, more and more avenues of employment, education, and participation that had previously been blocked to them — either through regulations or social norms — were opening up and accepting women into their ranks. In this way, militaries that follow this trend can be seen as keeping up with the wider society, and in general have better civil—military relations as a result. It has been observed, however, that the military as a social institution is often among the more conservative risk-averse, and hence among the slowest of such institutions to make this advancement. Compounding this factor is the nature of military life itself, as well as its traditional view of soldiers as warriors, and the longstanding western (and, it should be noted, East Asian) view of warriors being exclusively a role for men. Thus, admitting women into the ranks of warriors can have a stronger backlash from military traditionalists, who fear for the very collapse of the institution itself, compared to other fields that are not so predicated upon an ethic of masculinity. In short, it is a hard transition to make, and is not without its growing pains.

In the modern (pre-Cold War/1900–1945) military, women were generally excluded from military participation, as they had been throughout history. The main exception to this was in the role of nurses in World War I (WWI). During the Second World War, however, social changes – often formed by the war itself – were taking place at a quick pace. The manpower needs of the war famously opened up jobs in manufacturing and other sectors to women, because much of the male population had been conscripted and deployed. Mirroring these changes to the social fabric, military units were created especially to be staffed by women in uniform. These were, of course, completely separate divisions from their male counterparts', following the social mores of the time. Nevertheless, these advances, including the UK's Women's Auxiliary Air Force (WAAF), formed in 1939, the Canadian Women's Royal Canadian Naval Service (Wrens), and the US Women's Army Corps (WAC) formed in 1943, were meaningful as they represented the first substantial acceptance, not only by the military, but also by society, of women serving in uniform in these nations. History shows that gains made in social advancement are almost never given up, and after the war, these units became a permanent fixture of the military force structure; at least until the practice of having separate female-only divisions gave way to partial integration in the late modern (Cold War/1945–1990) military.

During the postwar period, women made slow but steady strides in gaining admittance to military ranks, at first in primarily support and clerical roles, but eventually a host of other avenues opened up to female participation. These included the officer corps in all branches of the military, as well as eventually all but combat roles. By the advent of the postmodern (post-Cold War/since 1990) military, virtually all military careers had been opened to women (largely still with the exception of combat roles), and the postmodern military began to conceive of itself as a gender-blind institution. In other words, individuals receive advancement and promotion based solely on their abilities and performance, and not on whether they are male or female. In reality, of course, this is far from the truth (Stewart, 2017).

There remain, even in the postmodern military, several lingering problems that stem from, or are exacerbated by, the issue of female participation in the military, not the least of which is the issue of sexual harassment. Many men, especially those attracted to the camaraderie and challenge of life as a warrior, seek to assert their masculinity in order to be accepted by the group, in part through sexual conquest, but even just in terms of locker room talk. Moreover, young men in a military environment and away from their homes for the first time find themselves without the social pressures that would otherwise hamper such behavior, and instead in a subculture that has traditionally encouraged it. While there are usually regulations that prohibit fraternization within the ranks, putting young men and women in such an environment together, away from home, it is inevitable that the result will include, in the most innocuous cases, dating and, in more extreme transgressions, sexual harassment. In a recent survey of 3,946 former US reservists, six out of every ten female respondents reported having faced incidents of harassment, compared to 27.2 percent of male respondents. Moreover, 13.1 percent of females (compared to 1.6 percent of males) reported having experienced sexual assault (Street, Stafford, Mahan, & Hendricks, 2008, p. 409). Part of the reason for this is in the merging of two cultures: that of a progressive society with that of the warrior, which for thousands of years has operated according to a traditional masculine ethic (Buchanan, Settles, Hall, & O'Connor, 2014).

Unfortunately, such statistics are often unreliable, as the studies they derive from are often agenda driven. For example, for the US DOD Sexual Assault Prevention Response Office 2012 Report, respondents were asked if they had ever been the victim of an unwanted sexual assault or contact: an important question, except that the wording of the question established the time frame for such incidents to include "up to a year prior to entering the military." Moreover, the survey defined certain innocuous behaviors, such as being asked out on a date, as "unwanted gender-related behavior" (United States Department of Defense, 2012). Despite agenda-driven research such as this, it is a commonly accepted fact that the rates of sexual assault and harassment within a military context exceed those of society in general, and this speaks in part to the aforementioned growing pains of having a traditionally male-dominated institution changing to accept females. It has been argued that female integration is a detriment to the cohesion and readiness of a military unit since small-unit cohesion is predicated on male bonding (Rosen, 2003, p. 325).

The topic of sexual harassment is often linked to that of women receiving special treatment, and the perception that women don't have to work as hard as their male counterparts in order to receive promotion, for example, or loading onto a course (McGuire, 2017). This happens in part because of good-faith efforts of the administration to help even out disparities and ensure females are represented at all levels of the chain of command to the fullest extent possible, but it can also happen through abuse of the sexual harassment safeguards through false reporting (Castro, Kintzle, Schuyler, Lucas, & Warner, 2015). This manipulation of sexual harassment protection rules can happen all too easily in an organization whose members have so little experience dealing with women as equals: in many traditional military environments, among that first generation tasked with dealing with female integration, the older male members can tend – even subconsciously – to view the female recruits as daughters, and seek to protect them. The younger males likewise tend to perceive the females as they have other women in their age cohort: potential sexual conquests (Lomsky-Feder & Sasson-Levy, 2016). Dropped into this environment, and told that being asked on an unwanted date constitutes sexual harassment, it is little wonder that women in uniform face statistically higher incidents of sexual harassment than their civilian colleagues, and when such harassment brings such severe penalties down upon its perpetrators, there is little wonder that the temptation to leverage these experiences can be so great. In the words of one serving female US military member, "Some of the harassment came from high-ranking officers. Over the years, I learned to use this to my advantage to make rank" (Smith, 2011).

While the phenomenon described above is by no means the rule, it can make it all the more difficult for female service members to gain acceptance as equals. And gaining acceptance and respect in a military group is not like doing so in other societal environments: it cannot be legislated, or even ordered. Respect must be earned. When lower standards and fast promotions make it easier for women to get the rank on their shoulders, it doesn't help them earn the respect of their peers, which is a necessary component of a properly functioning military unit (Kamarck, 2016). Conversely, women who serve in uniform and who receive no special treatment as a consequence of their gender, and who therefore have to compete equally with their male counterparts, are more likely to earn the respect of their peers and become fully accepted as "one of the lads" in the unit (King, 2015). In short, the issue of women in the military is a complicated one, requiring frank and open discussion in order to arrive at the truth.

1.1.9. Spouses and the Military Community

The postmodern military differs from its predecessor models in many salient ways, one of which − at the microlevel, or the level as perceived by the individual soldier − is the degree to which being a part of this organization is central to that soldier's identity. Moskos's institutional vs occupational (I/O) model describes how the institutional militaries are responsible for providing the good things in life − housing is on base, soldiers are fed, their bills paid, and their career path clear. In contrast, at the occupational end of the spectrum, wherein the military life is regarded more as a job than as a sacred calling, a soldier is like any other citizen: he is paid by his employer, and after work hours (which still do not always conform to the 9-to-5 model), his life is his own. Nowhere is this more obvious than in the role of spouses and their participation in military life.

Spouses − and by spouses, we mean predominantly wives − were an integral part of the modern (pre-Cold War/ 1900−1945) US military as they were called upon to take part in voluntary activities and social functions in life on the base. These spouses were never inducted into the military, of course, but by virtue of the fact that they were married to service members, they had a responsibility to represent and participate in the social life of the military community. This was perhaps more pronounced at the officer level, as well as with non-commissioned officers (NCOs) of the sergeant's rank and above. In contrast, the lower ranks were often unmarried, with much lower rates of marriage than in the larger society. This dynamic is perhaps not surprising — for one thing, the era coincides with a time when women had no role within the military itself, or that role was greatly circumscribed. In America, it also coincides with a time when a far smaller percentage of females worked outside the home in careers of their own, independent of their husbands'.

This integral role was reduced to partial involvement by the late modern (Cold War/1945—1990) military, as gender equality in society as a whole was slowly being realized and women had more educational, career, and lifestyle opportunities outside the home and separate from their husband's occupation. Not only did the greater number of empowered wives have less time to devote to playing the army wife on base, but also her identity was no longer dominated by that role. This trend continued to grow until spouses — and by this era we are no longer referring predominantly to civilian wives, but a greater number of civilian husbands, as well as spouses who themselves are service members — had become largely removed from participation in the postmodern (post-Cold War/since 1990) military.

1.1.10. Homosexuals in the Military

The issue of homosexuals serving in the military and the way this is treated by military and civilian leaders is at the heart of the postmodern military. The issue remains a controversial one, given the traditional nature of the military ethic, yet one that continues gradually to gain wider acceptance, following similar progress in wider society. In the modern (pre-Cold War/1900–1945) military, men found to be engaging in homosexual activity were most often punished for it, either officially through reprimands and jail time (they were often incarcerated during wartime, whereas in times of peace they would be discharged), or unofficially by their peers (Goldbach & Castro, 2016).

In times of mass conscription in the United States, as well as in much of the West, despite the need for bodies, there was an effort made to avoid having homosexuals serve in uniform, much less doing so openly. This would have been a drain on morale, and the soldier in question would not be able to earn the trust and respect of his comrades — essential qualities for a brother-in-arms. Thus, gay men, or even those who were particularly effeminate, were identified and removed from service, most often through a discharge for "inaptness or undesirable habits or traits of character" (as opposed to a straight-up honorable discharge). Of course, it was easier just to prevent homosexuals from joining, so instructions were issued to recruiters on how to identify gay men. These included feminine body characteristics, as well as attire and behavior that appeared effeminate (Laurence & Matthews, 2012, p. 347).

In the late modern (Cold War/1945–1990) military, homosexuals are still not tolerated within the ranks, the difference being that the punishment for homosexual behavior becomes less severe. In May 1951, the Uniform Code of Military Justice replaced the Articles of War in the United States, and it established sodomy as court martial offense. Treatment of homosexuals differs among postmodern (post-Cold War/since 1990) militaries in a way that is largely dependent on the culture of the nation in question. Much has been written about the American non-policy of "don't ask, don't tell" and the blowback from US President Bill Clinton's 1993 effort to have the prohibition lifted on gays in the US military. Meanwhile, though still not tolerant of it, the US military was generally more permissive on the issue than in the United Kingdom, for example, yet far more restrictive than the Canadian military and those of Scandinavia. This spectrum of experience stands as further evidence that the PMMM must be attenuated by the culture in which it is being applied, and is not a one-size-fits-all construct. In the context of a postmodern military, the various experiences also demonstrate that the issue of homosexuals serving in the armed forces may serve as an indicator of the alignment of the military to the society.

1.1.11. Conscientious Objection

The concept and practice of conscientious objection (CO), which refers to the right of an individual to refuse to perform military service on the grounds that it conflicts with his freedom of thought or conscience, dates to the sixteenth century, and has almost always been predicated on a provable religious conviction on the part of the individual claiming it. Dutch Mennonites were first granted exception from military service in 1575 by William of Orange, though they had to make up for their service in the form of a monetary payment. In the United States, CO has been recognized since the country's founding: many of the first settlers to the new world were those who had fled religious persecution in Europe and sought a place where they could live according to their beliefs. These communities, such as the Quakers, who were often at odds with the government in Britain over the issue of CO, became among the first Americans, and their desire not to take part in military activities was respected. Today, many of these Quaker and Mennonite communities, such as the Pennsylvania Amish, continue to live according to the old ways, forswearing the accoutrements of modern life, and they continued to be exempt from military service, even when the United States employed conscription.

Modern (pre-Cold War/1900–1945) militaries generally follow this pattern: limiting their permission of CO to members of religious orders that were well known as being dedicated to peace and nonviolence. In some nations, individuals claiming CO status had the option of serving in uniform, albeit in noncombat roles, or else going to prison. By the late modern (Cold War/1945–1990) military, alternative service channels such as civilian service were being established, and COs had a non-military option. Moreover, in this stage, there is wider acceptance of CO, again on religious grounds, but even now on the part of members of religious denominations that are not specifically pacifist, such as Protestantism and Catholicism. Individuals claiming a personal conviction however, in the absence of any religious reasons, were not so fortunate. The so-called draft dodgers during the Vietnam War are an example, and even today many such individuals continue to reside in Canada, though they were granted a general amnesty in 1977 by US President Jimmy Carter.

It was not until the postmodern (post-Cold War/since 1990) military that the regulations requiring a provable religious affiliation for exemption from duty became widespread and the notion of conscientious objection for secular and personal reasons gained more acceptance, albeit in systems that generally did not employ conscription. However, a new trend emerged in which serving military members, already in uniform and having voluntarily signed up, refused deployments to Iraq and Afghanistan on the grounds of conscientious objection. This truly postmodern trend represents a complex problem – the postmodern military had become one marked by occupational characteristics: Young people joined to attain skills, or get an education, or to escape a generational socio-economic pattern, and not necessarily to fight for country – and to be fair, this is how the recruiters would often sell it (McGlynn & Monforti, 2016). Suddenly, when ordered to deploy to a war zone, many of these individuals chose, as a generation ago, to run to Canada, where many remain today, unable to return to the United States. It should be pointed out that many of these individuals, having served their tour or two tours in the Middle East, found themselves on the receiving end of the US Army's "involuntary mobilization" orders, issued to thousands of members of the Individual Ready Reserve.

CHAPTER 2

ETHNIC SELF-IDENTIFICATION

The area of race, even ethnicity, is a charged one in public discourse in North America today, and one in which researchers must tread extremely carefully to avoid unintentionally offending the sensibilities of a public that is increasingly quick to take offense. This condition is particularly pronounced in academia, and perhaps because of this, there is distressingly little available research on issues of comparative ethnic identification. Rather, the concept of ethnic identity seems to be mostly viewed in isolation among discrete immigrant groups, rather than answering questions related to individual choices of ethnic self-identification.

There are a number of studies examining questions of ethnicity in Taiwan, especially as to how it is related to the conception of national identity.[1] According to Wu (2008), the 1990s saw ethnic relations in Taiwan coalesce into a binary framework of confrontation as what he terms the "burgeoning Taiwanese identity," which began to take shape and challenge the long-prevailing Chinese identity enforced by decades of authoritarian rule. This led to a polarization of ethnic consciousness that is the core of ethnic identification in the current study.

In most countries, only a small proportion of the population is of sufficiently mixed heritage as to be in the individual position to have a claim on one of a range of possible identities. For example, in the United States, there are a number of individuals with mixed-race parentages, such as having a Caucasian father and an African-American mother, and thus they are in the position in today's society to embrace that aspect of their racial heritage with which they most identify. Still, US census data for 2014 indicates that only about 45,672,250 people are African American, or African American in combination with another race, which accounts for a mere 14.3 percent of the US population, according to the National population and housing census (2014).

In contrast, in Taiwan, mixed-race heritage is not only more widespread, but it also is considered by many to be a defining characteristic of this population. Moreover, most previous studies look at ethnicity and ethnic identification within the context of a multicultural, multiethnic society such as the United States or Canada. The dynamic is extremely different in a largely homogeneous society (despite self-identification as either Mainlander or Taiwanese, both are, in strict racial terms, considered Han Chinese) such as that in Taiwan, and indeed most East Asian countries. These foreign studies are instructive in composing conceptualization and operationalization schemes (Whaley, 2005, p. 87; Williams & Thornton, 1998, p. 255).

On the issue of ethnic identification, Isajiw (1992) provides an excellent theoretical backgrounder as he identifies four main approaches: the primordialist, epiphenomenon, situational, and subjective approaches. The first of these looks at ethnicity as fixed and genetically determined. The other three arose as reactions to the established sociological and anthropological orthodoxy of looking at ethnicity as a primordial phenomenon. The epiphenomenon approach used a center-periphery model to conceptualize ethnicity, and posits that uneven patterns of economic disparity determine where ethnic groups consolidate and establish their culture. The situational approach, Isajiw points out, is based on rational choice theory in that people choose to identify with certain ethnic groups based on the perceived advantages that will be accrued as a result. This is similar to the instrumentalist approach, which is preferred by Hempel (2004). The subjective approach conceives of ethnicity as almost completely divorced from matters of culture or any concrete measuring as according to the primordialist school, and instead is a function of psychological "us vs them" perceptions and mutually accepted realities.

Other scholars have conceptualized ethnicity as multifaceted: A "mode of social differentiation based primarily on perceptions of kinship, a common cultural focus, and an awareness of historical destiny" (Bornman, 1999). This is actually an excellent definition for the various aspects making up the concept of "ethnic identity" in Taiwan today.

Using Social Identity Theory as a theoretical framework is a possible means of explaining the phenomenon.[2] Originally proposed by Henri Tajfel (1979) and John Turner (1982), membership groups could be anything from social class to a sports team, and provide a sense of pride and self-esteem to the individual. In Taiwan, for example, social groups may include ethnic groups such as Hakka or an indigenous group, or it may be expressed as *Benshengren* (本省人) or *Waishengren* (外省人). Young people in Taiwan today are under several sources of pressure that influences how they define themselves and their place in society: in a Confucian-influenced society, birth order, gender, and family characteristics are not the least of these (Yu & Su, 2006, p. 1059).

Furthermore, the way Taiwanese perceive their ethnic identity greatly impacts their political views: those identifying as Taiwanese, for example, may see China as a threat that promises to annex Taiwan and erase their ethnic distinctiveness by absorbing them into the greater Han majority. Those identifying as Mainlander (or Chinese in general), meanwhile, may not share this Taiwanese consciousness and generally envision an inevitable unification of Taiwan and China. How does each group regard the nation's armed forces? Ethnic identification is an essential element in the ROC citizen's emotional response to the mission to defend against China, and therefore a key concept in this study.

2.1. THE IDENTITY ISSUE IN TAIWAN

Identity is a contentious and ever-shifting issue in Taiwan, and as it is central to the thrust of this research, it is worth offering some words on the issue of identity in Taiwan today, how it is manipulated and portrayed in the media, and how the understanding of it continues to evolve thanks to ongoing work by a number of scholars.

Both the Chinese in China and those who identify as Chinese in Taiwan tend to view the Taiwanese (Minnan speakers) themselves as just another group of Han Chinese people. This is essentially true, from a primordialist perspective: the migration of Chinese people to Taiwan did not begin until the seventeenth century when the Dutch colonizers attracted (and in some cases, kidnapped) Chinese farmers from Fujian and Guangzhou provinces to work the plantations they had established.[3] Thus, the Taiwanese people today are the descendants of these and subsequent waves of immigration during the Qing dynasty, along with a high degree of intermarriage with the indigenous population.

Since the democratization era, much has been written about an "emerging Taiwanese identity" gaining ground on the island (Harrison, 2016). Moreover, this is often linked to the search for indigenous ancestors, blood, or DNA, as a means to cement one's Taiwanese bona fides (Tsai, 2014). In fact, the desire to find such genealogical evidence may be read as a rebuff of the Chinese identity that has been imposed upon Taiwan's people since 1949. Put simply, the interesting point is not that the Taiwanese don't see themselves as Chinese today: it's that they don't want to.

In late May 2016, the newspapers in Taiwan reported on a poll conducted by the Taiwanese Public Opinion Foundation in which 80 percent of respondents reported that they identified as Taiwanese, with a mere 8.1 percent identifying as Chinese (7.6 percent identified as both). This is in stark contrast to similar polls conducted in the late 1980s and early 1990s in which the vast majority reported identifying as Chinese or both. What happened in the short span of a single generation that could change an entire nation's self-perception so radically?

In fact, no such sea change ever took place. Indeed, neither historical roots nor system-level changes are sufficiently able to influence group identity on the scale of what has been measured (Chu, 2004, p. 498). Rather, according to researcher Frank Muyard (2012), what happened in the 1990s was not a rising Taiwanese identity, but rather an unraveling of the previous era's preference falsification, spurred by a newfound freedom to express an authentic sentiment on the issue of identity, including in polls. As with many oppressed and/or colonized peoples throughout the world and throughout history, the Taiwanese identity can be conceptualized in opposition to an external "other." Before the era of democratization, Taiwaneseness stood in opposition to the Kuomintang (KMT) and that party's authoritarianism, White Terror, and quasi-Leninist efforts to control all forms of social expression by subsuming Taiwaneseness into a subset of Chineseness. For evidence of the expression of this phenomenon one need look no further than the political accretion of opposition forces who chose the name Tangwai (黨外), or literally "outside the party."

In the 1990s, democratization opened up new avenues for exploring the idea of Taiwaneseness and what it means. Several things happened in the 1990s. First, the DPP established itself as a legitimate and legal alternative to the KMT and standard bearer of Taiwan-centered politics. The rise of democratic politics meant that the Taiwan identity could no longer be defined as resistance to the System: the Tangwai were now part of the system in the form of the DPP and its allies. Further, the KMT under Lee Tung-hui, who was president throughout the entire decade, co-opted many DPP programs and positions, and thus appeared to be Taiwanizing. That made it difficult to oppose the KMT as an anti-Taiwanese party (Wang & Liu, 2004, p. 577).

Survey results from the late 1980s and early 1990s show a high number of respondents identifying as Chinese because, according to Muyard (2012), the Taiwanese had long learned that it was safer to lie to the State. As society opened up through democratization and the end of the authoritarian era, people felt more comfortable publically admitting to a sense of Taiwaneseness, and telling the truth in such surveys. Therefore, there was no real "emergence" of a Taiwanese identity in the 1990s, but rather the uncloaking of a theretofore hidden one. Moreover, once people from Taiwan were finally able to visit China in the 1980s and 1990s, the stark contrast between the two cultures across the Taiwan Strait began to be made clear. Since the opening of Taiwan to thousands of Chinese tourists by the administration of former President Ma Ying-jeou, this process of differentiation has only accelerated due to close interpersonal contact (Turton, 2016).

Why is the identity issue so important? For one thing, it calls into question the appropriateness of any impulse to impose a Western form on the ROC military, such as the effort to transition to an AVF. Rather, a unique structure tailored to Taiwan's realities must be adopted. Again, the PMMM can assist in this effort, though not as a blueprint: rather as an analytical tool. What would be an appropriate disposition for the military of a postmodern society faced with an early-modern threat profile? This is the challenge facing Taiwan planners, and it is a challenge that will not be solved by simply importing institutional structures from the West. To answer that question, one must adopt a culturalist perspective.

2.2. A CULTURALIST PERSPECTIVE

The culturalist approach is not an easy or clean one for analysts to adopt, any more than it is for the theoreticians and scientists engaged in the study of comparative politics. What is required is an intersubjective cultural approach (Ross, 2009, p. 135), one defined by shared meanings and identities. Anthropologist Clifford Geertz's (1973) conception of culture famously focuses on symbols and symbolism to transmit meaning, with culture as a medium for shared meaning and meaning-making. The Confucian worldview is far from uniform across East Asia, but in broad strokes, it emphasizes the hierarchical makeup of the public administrative sphere (as this reflects the hierarchical makeup of the realm of heaven) and even extends to the family. Of the many spheres of human interaction that are moderated through the Confucian worldview, it is the Confucianism of the family, rather than

political Confucianism, that has formative power (Bell &
Jayasuriya, 1995, p. 9).

Familization is a familiar technique, often employed in
Taiwan, as a means of understanding and establishing rela-
tionships in group dynamics. The idea that members of a
collective are akin to a family is a subtle, psychological form
of control in which those in charge seek to be viewed as the
father figure, and are thus entitled to obedience in exchange
for protection of the community. This is exacerbated by the
lower but equally level-oriented roles of big brother, big
sister, younger brother, younger sister, and so forth, which
are transmitted primarily, though not exclusively, through
the Chinese language. In contrast, in America, the leader is
seen (most often inaccurately) as the antithesis of an elite,
and rather as a peer: one of many. Even compared to the
European practice of democracy, America's is far more individualistic and bottom-up. As a result, public governance
structures and operations reflect these divergent worldviews,
with Western structures moving toward a networked model,
and in Taiwan, toward one that is still very hierarchical. In
the words of Marc Ross (2009, p. 139), "culture frames the
context in which politics occurs."

The assertion that culture provides a framework for inter-
preting the actions and motivations of others (Ross, 2009,
p. 45) is an enlightening extension of this theme. On the
all-important issue of Taiwan's democracy, popular religious
expression provides an ideal blueprint for the development of
an informal political organization (Cohen, 1969, p. 217). It
has been noted by keen observers of Taiwanese culture that
the celebratory patterns in place for centuries used in temple
celebrations find expression in the exercise of democracy. It is
perhaps no surprise that, in a young democracy like Taiwan,
people should lean on existing, comfortable patterns of
communal interaction – those learned from the sphere of

religion — when developing new patterns for new social output, which is precisely what democratic expression was in the 1980s and 1990s. The result of this juxtaposition of forms and rituals is the unconscious conflation of democracy itself into an institution with the power and sacredness of a religion.

Clearly, the traditional society of Taiwan has evolved to accommodate quite well the attributes of democracy, respect for human rights, gender equality, and other concepts that can be described as modernized, all while maintaining the traditional values of hard work and filial piety that have contributed to what it means to be Taiwanese. It is therefore not a stretch to assert that the ROC military can likewise find a way to accommodate itself into this society — a task that it has thus far been unable to achieve. As the current research shows, the people of Taiwan want a military that reflects the values of their society. What problems exist (public attitude, poor media coverage) can be attributed largely to this gulf of values.

NOTES

1. Unfortunately, much of this research tends to extend into the political realm, making it difficult to find work that is not conducted in service of a political agenda.

2. According to Social Identity Theory, the concept of social identity is related to the method by which an individual tends to develop a sense of self by using as a foundation his or her membership in a larger group.

3. While the indigenous populations were already accomplished farmers, they preferred subsistence farming, and were resistant to being made into taxable subjects, yet the Dutch needed a dependent workforce that would produce a surplus — this workforce they imported from China.

CHAPTER 3

THREAT PERCEPTION IN TAIWAN

The threat perception that drives the ROC military and society is that of attack from China. This puts Taiwan's military in the era of a modern military, or akin to what was experienced by much of the West in the pre-Cold War era. Yet the precise nature of the threat is unlike the examples in the West that served as the inspiration for Moskos et al. as they developed the PMMM. Unlike, for example, the nation-states of Europe that experienced centuries of invasion and attack in a pattern that persisted right up until the Second World War, the enemy in the cross-strait scenario is not an alien, foreign invader: The Chinese in China consider the people of Taiwan to be their cousins, albeit distant cousins. There is no desire to slaughter a hated enemy, as is often the case between the feuding nationalisms of pre-Cold War Europe. It should be noted that this affinity is also a factor in why there is virtually no fear in Taiwan of a nuclear attack by China, despite Beijing having a sizeable arsenal of nuclear weapons. Neither the pundits, the analysts, nor the people see this as a realistic possibility, and therefore the assessment of this dimension remains within the modern era, without having progressed to the late modern.

Moreover, many of those Taiwan citizens with Mainlander parents, as well as those identifying as Chinese, do not tend to consider China a threat at all, or if they do, prefer to couch it in terms of there being a threat from "an outside country." This would seem to support the view that Mainlanders and their descendants on Taiwan who still view themselves as Chinese have a closer affinity to the Chinese in China than they do to the Taiwanese in Taiwan. A more thorough analysis of this dimension would take these cultural indicators into account, in qualifying the exact nature of the threat, which may factor into the motivation for the threat. On this last point, the motivation for China's desire to annex Taiwan is not driven solely by geopolitics or resource acquisition so much as a desire to win the last battle of the Chinese Civil War by defeating the KMT. It is as much an emotional imperative as a political one, and this only becomes apparent by taking a culturalist approach.

The threat of annexation by China overshadows all others. There still exist, however, the postmodern threats that face other nations today: Islamic terrorism, for example, remains always on the radar, especially as Taiwan's sole security guarantor, the United States, has been preoccupied with this particular threat (almost to the exclusion of all others) since 9-11, which means that there is pressure from Washington for its allies to likewise shift their focus to the war on terror. Outside of the largely theoretical possibility of an Islamic terrorist strike on Taiwan soil or targeted at ROC citizens, however, there is little else that comes close to the ever-present China threat in the public's consciousness.

Moreover, the nature of the China threat has enormous implications not just for force structure within the ROC military, but also for society as a whole. This is because, unlike previous threat paradigms, the China threat is not restricted to force of arms and military matters, but rather encompasses other facets of nation-to-nation interaction. While the current disparity between Taiwan and China — in military and economic terms — has forced ROC planners to adopt an asymmetrical approach to defense, it is perhaps ironic that China's approach is also asymmetrical, largely as a result of Chinese planners configuring their assets and responses with an eye to fighting the United States: a military disparity of another scale.

Following the doctrine of Unrestricted Warfare first enunciated in 1999 by People's Liberation Army (PLA) Colonels Qiao Liang and Wang Xiangsui, China has succeeded in creating the conditions whereby its economic and supply-chain integration with Taiwan's economy can be used as a weapon to coerce capitulation. In addition to the economic sphere, Chinese attempts to effect rapprochement on Beijing's terms take many forms, including cultural (promoting the idea that the Taiwanese are the descendants of Yan and Yellow Emperor), electronic (PLA hackers are constantly launching cyberattacks on Taiwan's government and corporate websites and servers, often as a means to test out new techniques before using them on American targets (Gold, 2013)), and covert (Chinese intelligence operatives have managed to turn many current and former military members, as well as civilians), among others. As a result, the threat from China as perceived in Taiwan exists on several fronts: political, diplomatic, cultural, economic, as well as military. In order to counter this threat, ROC defense planners developed and implemented the concept of "All-out Defense," which conceptualizes national defense as a task to be carried out by the whole of society, and not just resting on the shoulders of the military.

Nontraditional security factors defining the China threat range from currency policy to economic integration and trade: from Beijing's efforts to help shape a regional order through multilateral institutions to a "culture war" (that Beijing and its proxies are waging – and losing – in Taiwan) to convince the people of Taiwan that their identity is a Chinese one, not Taiwanese.

3.1. THREAT PERCEPTION AMONG TAIWANESE "MAINLANDERS"

The issue is threat perception, with the emphasis on perception. This complicates the issue somewhat in Taiwan due to the fact that various subgroups of Taiwan society have different perceptions of identity, and thus, different views on Taiwan's place in the larger Sinophonic world. The implications of this result in two divergent conceptions of just what the threat from China entails.

Persons in Taiwan who self-identify as Mainlanders by and large see themselves as Chinese. They see few differences between their cultural inheritance and the cultural inheritance of the people of China. Except for what social changes have evolved between the peoples across the Taiwan Strait over the past six decades, Mainlanders believe that they are, in essence, the same culture. Indeed, in the early years of the separation, the evacuees of 1949 saw themselves and the KMT regime as being the more authentically Chinese: it was not only a political slogan that the ROC was the "real China" or "Free China," it was a social conception. Not only did Republican China's institutions, both governmental and social, transplant themselves to Taiwan after the Communist takeover of the mainland, but the regime became, by necessity, the guardian of the ages-old Chinese culture. This was only given impetus by events taking place on the mainland, such as the Great Leap Forward and, more importantly, the

Cultural Revolution, in which millions of Chinese people died and entire traditions and ways of life were wiped out in the Communist zeal to remake society in the Party's image.

This unbroken lineage of a Confucian worldview serving as a guide to life among the people of Taiwan puts them in direct contrast with those in China. The Chinese Communist Party attempted to purge the *Great Sage* and erase his lessons and legacy from the everyday lives of Chinese people. As the era of Mao Zedong wore on into the decade of the 1970s, an ardent anti-Confucius campaign was launched as part of the larger-scale Great Proletarian Cultural Revolution that tried to erase the cultural and social traditions that had existed in China for millennia, and to replace them with the ideological precepts of Marxism. The "Criticize Lin (Biao), Criticize Confucius" campaign ran from 1973 to 1974 and was started by Mao's third wife, Jiang Qing. Meanwhile, Karl Marx was being worshiped by socialists in no less real a way than Confucius had been worshiped by Chinese: as far as his followers were concerned, Marx was the new sage.

In contrast, through the efforts of the KMT regime, Taiwan has served as a reliquary of sorts for this Han cultural inheritance even as it was being actively and violently dismantled across the strait. Even more than that, there are many within the old guard of the KMT who still believe that the party continues to hold the Mandate of Heaven, which it earned in 1912 with the fall of the Qing dynasty and the establishment of the ROC. This ancient Chinese belief in the *tiānmìng* (天命), or "heaven's decree," is part of a worldview which perceives the structure of government on earth as reflecting the structure in heaven, and that heaven itself has always granted emperors the right to rule, based largely on their ability to govern fairly. Since the ROC has been in continuous existence since the end of the Qing dynasty, this mantle has never been passed on to the Communist regime in

China, and thus it is still held by the KMT. Of course, this concept is hardly a driving force in policymaking, nor is it forefront in the minds of Taiwan's leaders who consider themselves Mainlanders. Nevertheless, it does inform, even at a subconscious level, their worldview and their duties as the gatekeepers of this inheritance and this responsibility. They are, to sum up, Chinese, not Taiwanese.

Now that the Mao era is over, the leaders of the Communist party have turned China into a capitalist state, albeit one in which the party still holds the reins. Moreover, since the death of Chiang Kai-shek, much of the anti-Communist fervor has dissipated and more practical approaches to cross-strait relations have prevailed. What remains is a population of very powerful and influential, albeit numerically disadvantaged, people in Taiwan who conceive of themselves as Chinese and who long to effect a return to their ancestral lands. Annexation of Taiwan by China is therefore not an existential threat to them − not in the way that decla-ration of a "Republic of Taiwan" would be. In essence, a dis-solution of the ROC in favor of a victory of the Taiwanese identity is a much greater threat to the conception of "Taiwan as China." Thus, those aspects of PRC efforts to manipulate Taiwan society by promoting a conception of shared Chineseness is readily embraced by some members of the self-identified mainlander population. Therefore, the China threat, in the eyes of Mainlanders, is in many ways a continuation of the Chinese Civil War, fought between the CCP and the KMT, for control of China − for the Mandate of Heaven.

3.2. THE CULTURE WAR

Leaders have always used different interpretations of Taiwanese history to advance agendas and control the population

(Hsiau, 2000, p. 157). Today, the competing visions of national identity play out in the culture war. On one side, the Mainlander faction sees Taiwan as part of China and goes to great lengths to organize events and exhibitions that celebrate the images and values of Chinese culture, and to emphasize the line of continuity from the ancient China of thousands of years ago to the Han Chinese people of Taiwan today. This faction, which until recently has held almost absolute power in Taiwan and has been the dominant power broker for much of the post-Japanese-colonial period, is collaborating in this effort with forces across the strait, simply because they genuinely share this vision. The PRC does not want to risk alienation in the international community by launching an exercise in military adventurism in order to annex Taiwan. Therefore, it must compel the Taiwanese to willingly give themselves over to the center of the Chinese world: Beijing. To do this, the PRC knows that the growing sense of Taiwanese identity is a threat, and it spares no expense to help its allies on the island to win the culture war and consolidate a widespread sense of Chinese identity in Taiwan.

On the other side, the Taiwanese, or those with a benshengren identity, exhibit a political expression that is traditionally seen as having accreted in the pan-green coalition of political parties that, directly or indirectly, support Taiwanese sovereignty and presumably eventual formal independence from China. Proponents of this camp organize cultural and social exhibitions and events that aim to inculcate a widespread sense of pride in Taiwan and everything that distinguishes the island from China. To them, the threat from China is also being waged on the cultural front.

Ironically, however, the closer Taiwan becomes with China in terms of increased levels of economic integration, trade, tourism, and cultural exchanges, the stronger the sense of Taiwan identity becomes. National Chengchi University's

Election Study Center has, since 1992, annually conducted a poll as part of an ongoing study on political attitudes, national identity, and the unification-independence issue. It is widely regarded as one of the most accurate and methodologically sound polls on this issue in Taiwan, where other such surveys are often suspect due to ideological bias. In 2015, results indicated that 23.9 percent of respondents supported independence, with 60.6 percent identifying as Taiwanese. This is a significant upward change since the 17.6 percent self-identifying as Taiwanese in 1992 (Taipei Times, 2015, p. 1). The 2015 numbers also registered a record-low 32.5 percent of respondents self-identifying as both Taiwanese and Chinese, which is down from 47.7 percent in 2004. Meanwhile, just 3.5 percent of respondents reported identifying as Chinese, down from 1994's 26.2 percent. It is important to note that this shift has taken place in an era when the door has been opened to China in terms of tourism, greater economic and trade exchanges, and more people-to-people interactions than had taken place in the previous century. This is why the push by both the KMT and the CCP to foment a sense of shared Chineseness by the peoples across the strait is not gaining purchase in Taiwan.

3.3. PUBLIC PERCEPTION OF THREAT

Given this background, one might expect that citizens of Taiwan would perceive an attack from China as being the main threat facing Taiwan today. Public perception, however, is more nuanced. Survey respondents with Chinese parents (Mainlanders), as well as those who self-identify as Chinese, were significantly more likely to phrase the threat as being from "another country" (i.e., a country other than Taiwan) as shown in **Figure 3.1**. This raises interesting questions

Figure 3.1. Threat Perception.

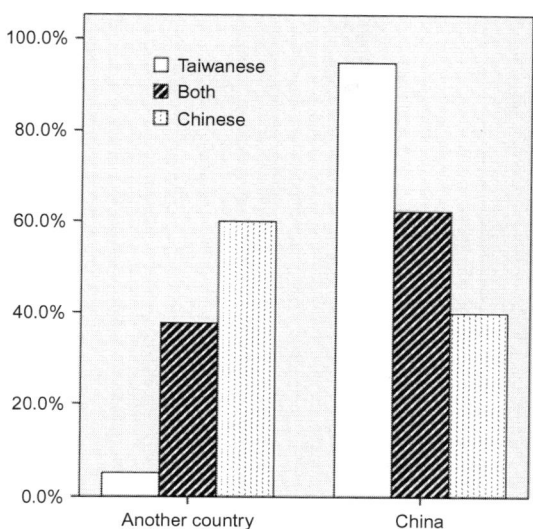

about causality: results show identity and threat are related, but is it an identity that changes threat perception or is it threat perception that influences identity? One might assume that identity is more or less fixed and constant, whereas threat perception is given to variability according to political and military events, making it more likely that the former would have an influence on the latter. However, in the case of Taiwan, the opposite might also be true.

Turner (1982) posits that individuals define themselves according to social relations and in comparison to an "other," and that this takes place at different levels of abstraction. Thus, the depth of the Taiwanese identity may be reinforced by being in opposition the "other" represented by China and the Chinese, which currently present a threat to

Taiwaneseness. Moreover, the dynamic may go both ways and form a self-reinforcing feedback loop, with the growing Chinese antagonism toward Taiwan contributing to a stronger Taiwanese identity, and that Taiwanese identity perceiving an increasingly greater threat from China, and so on.

Whatever the mechanism, there are doubtless cultural reasons for these results. While those who identify as Taiwanese, and who presumably share some degree of Taiwanese consciousness, are not afraid to name the threat as being China, those who identify as Chinese still recognize the same threat, but prefer to frame it in abstract terms. By taking this one step back from outright naming it, it may be psychologically safer for self-identified Mainlanders to ascribe the threat to an unnamed "other country" than it is to ascribe the threat to the group across the Taiwan Strait with a shared heritage.

These results speak to the schism in Taiwan society as regards the perceived threat from China, and one that makes a PMMM assessment of the nation's military an exercise that requires great nuance. The PMMM was designed to explain events transpiring in the evolution of armed forces in Western nations, particularly in the Cold War era, and it was framed with certain assumptions, among those being that its conception of "threat of enemy invasion" as described for the modern through the late-modern phases was indeed a threat from an enemy. Here we see indications that, while the perception of a threat of invasion remains, for at least a portion of the population (and one which has largely framed the societal narrative), the threat is not always perceived as being from an "enemy."

Likewise, persons who have an ethnic self-identification as Chinese are significantly less likely to worry about the China threat than their counterparts who identify as Taiwanese (Table 3.1). To understand why this is so, it is helpful to conceptualize what exactly is being threatened. Should a Chinese

Table 3.1. Cross-Strait Worry: One-By-One Correlations.

	Ethnic Self-identification[a]	Parents' Ethnic Background[b]	Position on Unification/Independence[c]	Threat Perception[d]	Cross-strait Worry[e]
Ethnic self-identification[a]					
Pearson Correlation	1	0.354**	−0.626**	−0.430**	0.134**
Sig. (2-tailed)		0.000	0.000	0.000	0.003
N	500	500	440	484	496
Parents' ethnic background[b]					
Pearson Correlation	0.354**	1	−0.319**	−0.261**	0.119**
Sig. (2-tailed)	0.000		0.000	0.000	0.008
N	500	501	440	484	496
Position on Unification/Independence[c]					
Pearson Correlation	−0.626**	−0.319**	1	0.459**	−0.258**
Sig. (2-tailed)	0.000	0.000		0.000	0.000
N	440	440	440	426	436

Table 3.1. (*Continued*)

	Ethnic Self-identification[a]	Parents' Ethnic Background[b]	Position on Unification/Independence[c]	Threat Perception[d]	Cross-strait Worry[e]
Threat perception[d]					
Pearson Correlation	−0.430**	−0.261**	0.459**	1	−0.273**
Sig. (2-tailed)	0.000	0.000	0.000		0.000
N	484	484	426	484	481
Cross-strait worry[e]					
Pearson Correlation	0.134**	0.119**	−0.258**	−0.273**	1
Sig. (2-tailed)	0.003	0.008	0.000	0.000	
N	496	496	436	481	496

**Correlation is significant at the 0.01 level (2-tailed).

[a] Taiwanese = 1, both = 2, Chinese = 3.

[b] Neither parent from mainland = −2, one parent from mainland = 0, both parents from mainland = 2.

[c] Unification = 1 to Independence = 5.

[d] Threat is China = 1, Threat is a country other than Taiwan = 0.

[e] Are you very worried = 1, to are you not worried = 4.

attack on Taiwan be carried out, and Taiwan annexed to the mainland, what does each group stand to lose?

How do those who identify as Chinese see the consequences of an attack from China? In the case of Mainlanders and others who self-identify as Chinese, being attacked and colonized by a Chinese power would not greatly affect their view of themselves or their group. Certainly they would not be as deeply affected as if the threat were coming from a culturally different source. Let us take Japan as an example: there is, of course, an historical precedent, when Taiwan was ceded by the Qing Court to the Empire of Japan in 1895. Within a generation, the (formerly) Chinese inhabitants of Taiwan were being educated to speak Japanese; they wore Japanese clothing and lived largely Japanese lifestyles. Indeed, neither being ethnically Japanese nor subjects of the Qing dynasty, it was during this era that the spark of a Taiwanese consciousness first appeared as the subject population sought to define itself. Thus the cultural identity that a Mainlander in Taiwan adheres to – that of being part of the Chinese culture – would not be threatened if the island is taken over by China, at least not as much as it would be if the island were taken over by another culturally different power.

How do those who identify as Taiwanese see the consequences of an attack from China? This is a very different threat perception among the Taiwanese population, who view annexation by China in much the same way as their Mainlander counterparts would see annexation by Japan in the thought experiment aforementioned. Persons self-identifying as Taiwanese do not view themselves as being culturally the same as the people across the Taiwan Strait, having grown apart from them (in a cultural sense) over the past 120 years that they have been separated.[1] Moreover, after Taiwan's long history of being colonized by one alien

power after another – from the Dutch and Spanish, to
Koxinga, and then the Manchu dynasty; by the Japanese;
and finally by the KMT (for being colonized is how many
Taiwanese writers perceive the ROC period (Au, 2008,
p. 65)) – finally the inhabitants of the island have the opportunity to chart their own future, and enjoy a newfound sovereignty and identity separate from that of any colonizing
power: thus the prospect of being colonized by China is
anathema, and therefore a much greater perceived threat for
them than for Mainlanders.

The PMMM assumes that a foreign power threatening
invasion follows the pattern, an almost universal one, wherein
motivation is to acquire land, power, or otherwise express
a rationalist approach to geopolitics and war wherein one
power hopes to decimate another power and take what it pos-
sesses. As we have seen, in the case of the cross-strait conflict,
there is much more at play, and much more that demands an
examination of the cultural conditions coloring the relationship. As described previously, the Mainlander faction in
Taiwan largely sees China and the Chinese as cousins, if
distant, but nevertheless related and hence less of a threat as it
is another party that shares its desire to unify, as all families
should. Likewise, the communist party leadership in China,
which could hardly be more different politically than the
democracy in Taiwan, see the population of the island
(Mainlander and Taiwanese both) as Chinese, and therefore
in need of being brought back into the fold and "reunified."
Therefore, the threat is largely a geopolitical one, and not
genocidal in that the Chinese do not desire to wipe out the
people of Taiwan.[2]

While the threat of invasion from China would situate
this dimension in the modern stage, the situation is not so
straightforward. There may be a host of other factors at play
here to help explain the phenomenon behind the survey

results obtained, and certainly further psychological and sociological research is called for to provide an in-depth explanation. What is abundantly clear at this stage, however, is that threat perception is not uniform across the ethnic groups making up Taiwan's population, and therefore the dimension of threat perception in Taiwan cannot be evaluated as cleanly as it can in most cases where the PMMM is applied.

NOTES

1. A common analogy to illustrate this feeling of distinctness is to point out that, while America was founded as a British colony, it would be disingenuous and wrongheaded to assert that Americans are, either culturally or politically, British. They manifestly are not.

2. Indeed, Beijing largely sees itself as a potential liberator for the people of Taiwan, seeking to once again and forevermore bring them into the greater Chinese family.

CHAPTER 4

FORCE STRUCTURE AND CONSCIENTIOUS OBJECTORS

4.1. FORCE STRUCTURE

Force structure is an important aspect of determining whether a military falls into the category of postmodern. It is concerned with the allocation of officers and men and the relationship between military units; it is influenced by the threat perception and designed to meet the established mission requirements. When threat perception is dominated by the threat of invasion, as during the modern era (roughly 1900–1945), a military is concerned primarily with the size of its standing army. This usually means the conscription of all or most of a nation's able-bodied young men for a period of national service.

The practice of conscription is by no means a product of the modern-era army, but rather one that goes back, in the western tradition, to the Babylonian Empire and, in the East, to the Qin Dynasty (221–206 BC). Indeed, even the pre-Qin era saw forced conscription in areas where peasants were recruited to fill out the ranks. In addition to serving a year in the military police, or "Zheng Zu (正卒)," to defend the Qin capital Xianyang, young conscripts (those aged 23 and up were eligible for the draft) were also required to serve for a year defending the frontier as a garrison troop, or "Shu Zu (戍卒)." This is in addition to the month-long duty "Geng Zu (更卒)," defending one's home county (睡虎地秦墓竹簡).

By the age of the Han dynasty (206 −220 BCE), this system largely continued as described earlier, with another parallel system evolving, in which all men aged between 15 and 56 years were subject to a system of corvée, or unpaid labor, one month per year. This system was discontinued in the Three Kingdoms Period (220−280 CE) in favor of private regional militias (shibingzhi世兵制), or hereditary conscription, wherein local governors could raise an army through recruitment of professional soldiers and prisoners of war. While there remained some press-ganging, peasants were largely freed of the obligation to take up arms.

The Sui dynasty (581−618 AD) and Tang dynasty (618−906 AD) employed a practice called the FuBing militia system (府兵制), in which men between the ages of 21 and 60 years would serve as a soldier (for a period of time determined by their distance from the capital) and, while not serving, they would work parcels of land which they had been assigned. It was during the Tang dynasty that an official, Duke Wenzhen of Yan (燕文貞公), initiated an end to conscription due to the rampant abuses perpetrated upon the soldiers and their families, and the widespread desertion that occurred as a result. He favored a system of recruitment of professional armed forces and paid higher salaries, and employing such managed to fill out the ranks.

In one form or another, conscription was practiced by the Song, Yuan, Ming, and Qing dynasties, as well as the modern-era Republican army. From 1927 to 1937, the ROC Armed Forces went through a period of modernization made possible due to assistance from foreign — mostly German — military advisors, including Max Bauer, Hans von Seeckt, and Alexander von Falkenhausen, who helped to reorganize ROC forces along the German model. These German advisors recommended that the large standing army[1] be replaced with a more professional type of soldier. For one thing, German military thinkers of the day were averse to the use of the very sort of large, conscription-based land forces that were heavily favored by Chinese military planners, and the advisors failed to implement this change. It would not be until 2008 that the ROC military would again seriously consider transforming from a draft-based force to one built upon professional soldiering.

Despite the attempts to transition the ROC military to an All-Volunteer Force, conscription remains the only viable form of ensuring sufficient manpower, and this is in large part why the ROC military is consistent with a modern (pre-Cold War) military in this dimension. Despite the effort by the military to make the AVF transition during the Ma administration, this remains a goal that is not shared by the people of Taiwan, who would prefer to keep conscription. Indeed, the persistent threat of attack from China, with its increasingly powerful and well-equipped PLA and the hundreds of missiles pointed at Taiwan, is a strong argument for keeping the draft, rather than rushing headlong into a model of a professional military staffed by recruitment simply because this is what advanced nations do.

4.2. FORCE STRUCTURE IN THE ROC

Force structure has shifted significantly in the ROC military in the years since 1949. In the 1950s, when Taiwan's population ranged from 8 to 11 million, the ROC military had a force of approximately 600,000 active frontline personnel. Today, although the population has swollen to 23.4 million, there is about half that number, with an active reserve force personnel of 1,675,000, at least on paper (2016 World Military Powers). Moreover, military spending amounted to almost half of total governmental expenditures in the 1950s, as the KMT geared up for an invasion to retake the mainland. Much of this shift can be attributed to the concomitant shift in mission definition, from the aforementioned invasion of China to defense of the island. It can also be attributed to the United States taking on the role of security guarantor (as America did for many nations and regions, freeing up financial resources in countries such as Japan and South Korea to focus on building successful economies as Washington took up the burden of paying for their defense).

The US advisors that were part of the Joint Commission on Rural Reconstruction (JCRR)[2] insisted that the Chiang regime give up its goal of retaking the mainland, and thus the military development that was creating such a budgetary burden. In late 1954, the two countries had signed the Sino-American Mutual Defense Treaty, which effectively solidified America's role as the ROC's security guarantor and allowed the KMT regime to reduce military expenditures, and arguably prevented either side in the Taiwan Strait conflict from taking over the other for the next two decades (Rubinstein, 2013, p. 31). The US role in safeguarding Taiwan's security has allowed for a steady decline of military spending as a share of total ROC government expenditures, dropping from over 40 percent in the 1960s to about 11 percent today (Templeman, Uzonyi, & Flores, 2015, p. 4).

The amount of military spending fell consistently from the era of the Joint Defense treaty (roughly 1949—1978), through the self-defense era (1979—1986) and to the era of democratic transition (1987—1996). Not only did this trend continue into the democracy era (1997–present), but the quality of personnel, training, and readiness fell as well, due largely to a decline in threat perception and a decline of the military's social role (Chen, 2009, p. 8).

In the joint defense stage, the ROC military was very much representative of the modern military form, defined by the threat of external invasion and a mission definition of defending against such an invasion and thus the focus on maintaining a large standing army. Regime survival was by no means a foregone conclusion in the 1950s. More than 100,000 soldiers were stationed on the frontline islands of Kinmen and Matsu, as these were widely considered the most likely target for a first strike from China. Indeed, in those early years, the first and second Taiwan Strait crises saw the ROC and PRC clash, largely in the form of bombardment campaigns. During the self-defense era, the ROC's loss of international diplomatic recognition did not greatly affect the force structure, except for a continuation of the size reductions, as well as reductions in military expenditures. This is despite the fact that this era saw the major mission definition change from one of preparing for an invasion to liberate the mainland, to one of a strictly defensive nature. Despite the end of the Joint Defense treaty with the United States, America remained Taiwan's security guarantor, in the form of the Taiwan Relations Act (TRA). Enacted by the US Congress in response to US President Jimmy Carter's derecognition of Taipei in favor of Beijing, the TRA compels the administration to sell defensive weapons to Taiwan in order to aid the island in defending itself against a Chinese attack, and according to some interpretations, promises a US military response to defend Taiwan from any such attack, provided it isn't instigated by a declaration of independence.

Chiang Ching-kuo put an end to 38 years of martial law in 1987, opening the door to the democratization era and a reevaluation of how the military was structured and run. In addition to increased calls for civilian control over the military, voices urged the localization of government institutions, including the armed forces. Five years after martial law was lifted, the government embarked on an armed forces reorganization project with the target of restructuring troop deployments and reducing the size of the standing army to half a million. This plan was soon replaced, however, by the promulgation of a Force Modification Plan — a streamlining project that called for a further reduction of force size to 400,000 (Edmonds & Tsai, 2006, p. 194). This reduction in military size was happening concurrently with a reduction in the military's clout within the party. Whereas serving officers once accounted for between two and five seats on the KMT Central Standing Committee, as well as several seats on the party's Central Committee, this influence was greatly reduced after a reshuffle (Chen, 2009, p. 37). The party—military relationship changed dramatically during this era, with the disengagement of the military from the party leadership structure, and hence that of the State, as well as increased civilian control over the military. In addition, the Taiwan Garrison Command, which was the arm of the military that served as frontline troops during the White Terror period, was dissolved in July 1992, separating the police forces of the island from military control. Finally, the removal of General Hau Pei-tsun, an influential military and party leader, from the core of political power in 1993 after his resignation from the premiership represented the beginning of the end of the quasi-Leninist party—state system in Taiwan and the normalization of society—military relations (Alagappa, 2001, p. 150).

While these and other military restructuring projects and programs have made detailed changes one way or the other, the big picture has always remained: Taiwan's is a conscript-based military. In terms of public perception, the current research shows that attitudes toward military conscription are associated significantly with self-identification. While it is clear that the vast majority (by a ratio of 3 to 1) want the ROC government to keep conscription, this support varies with education level and ethnic identification. Specifically, the higher a person's education, the less likely that person is to support conscription. While this is not necessarily germane to a culturalist perspective (as levels of education are unrelated to ethnic self-identification), it is worth noting, and seeking an explanation. It is likely that those who have themselves benefited from the higher education system in Taiwan see conscription as a throwback to a less enlightened, less globalized age. Moreover, such education often brings with it a degree of worldliness, and a desire for Taiwan society to be more akin to the advanced nations of the world – to be more democratic, more egalitarian, and less provincial. Continued conscription is an impediment to these aspirations. Interestingly, the more educated the respondent, the more worried they are about the military threats from the PRC. This simultaneous worry among the higher educated about the threat from China yet dislike of conscription suggests that the nation's educated elites may not see the military – or at least, not a large standing army – as the key to solving the cross-strait impasse. What that key is, however, is a question that begs further research (**Figure 4.1**).

More relevant to our examination of the PMMM, however, are the results concerning the relationship between views on conscription and ethnicity. The results show that the more one identifies as Taiwanese, the greater the odds the respondent will prefer to end conscription. Moreover, in terms of the reasons for their views, only identity is significant, with a higher identification as Chinese tending to view conscription as being "good for youth." Conversely, identifying as Taiwanese increases the odds of "the China threat"

Figure 4.1. Preferred Conscription Policy.

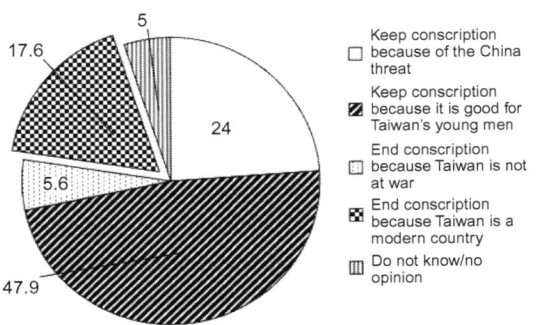

□	Keep conscription because of the China threat
▨	Keep conscription because it is good for Taiwan's young men
▢	End conscription because Taiwan is not at war
⊠	End conscription because Taiwan is a modern country
▥	Do not know/no opinion

being used as a reason for keeping conscription. As discussed, those identifying as Chinese have a lower perception of a threat from China, and hence it is logical that they would not prefer to keep conscription due to a China threat, but rather because it is good for the youth.

In sum, both the China threat and an improved image of the army concur to promote conscription across the board, regardless of what reason is given. This has policy implications for the ROC government as it wrestles with efforts to transition to an AVF. This also has lessons for military planners as they seek to make today's military in Taiwan more relevant to all of society, and not merely a portion of it. A large part of the military's role in the early days of the KMT regime in Taiwan was to provide indoctrination into party philosophy among the nation's youth. The ROC military was essentially the military arm of the KMT, and it remained so during the de facto one-party state ruled by the KMT in Taiwan, wherein the political indoctrination it provided aided to ensure the loyalty of its members, and political officers and commissioners were installed in each company to monitor that loyalty. This latter practice was employed initially by Chiang Kai-shek and Chiang Ching-kuo as a means of ensuring loyalty to the KMT at a time when Communist agents and sympathizers routinely infiltrated the ranks of the armed forces, and entire frontline units are known to have defected to the PRC. It is therefore not surprising that persons identifying as Mainlanders perceive of conscription as worth keeping because it is good for the nation's youth: especially now that the nation's youth are increasingly identifying as Taiwanese and – more distressingly for those who identify as Chinese – are becoming increasingly emboldened in their opposition to the way in which the KMT administered Taiwan's democratic institutions. This trend, of course, culminated in the Sunflower Movement in which a group of activists made up largely of students seized control of the Legislative Yuan and occupied that building from March 18 to April 10, 2014. This eventuality would surely never have happened had more of today's youth been indoctrinated into the philosophies espoused by the military system in days past, which included a heavy dose of respect for one's elders.

4.3. CONSCIENTIOUS OBJECTORS IN THE ROC MILITARY

The alternative service channels that allow young men of conscription age to avoid donning the uniform in favor of performing some other, non-military service puts Taiwan in the postmodern category in this dimension. However, the lack of combat deployments in the past several decades means that commitment to conscientious objection has not been put to the test, the way it has for example in the US military, when even volunteer soldiers declared themselves Conscientious

Objectors (CO) after receiving orders to deploy in the First Gulf War (Robinson, 2016, p. 107).

The issue of conscientious objection is one that has received little attention in Taiwan — either by the military itself or by society at large — for most of the post-war period. Administratively, it is not the defense ministry, but rather the Ministry of the Interior, that is responsible for conscription and related issues. Moreover, the topic is one that is viewed very differently in the East Asian context, compared to how it is viewed in the West, incorporating facets of equality and religion (Chen, 2009, p. 92).

Like its western counterparts, the ROC Constitution hews to the principle of equality for all under the law, regardless of religion, gender, or race (Article 7). Unlike in the West, however, the way society interprets this is less about rights and more with a focus on responsibilities. Indeed, Chapter II is subtitled "Rights and Duties of the People" (emphasis own). This, combined with the military service obligation promulgated in Article 20 and the Act of Military Service System (in effect since 1933), form the legal basis for universal male conscription in the ROC.

The Confucian-influenced values upon which Taiwan society is based are often cited for widespread societal acceptance of conscription: predicated on that belief-system's stipulations regarding duty to family, as well as to society, in a social system that is often familized and thus which benefits from feelings of filial duty. This sense of duty, and the lack of any widespread grassroots agitation for a reevaluation of conscription, may be exacerbated by the ever-present threat of invasion from China. Thus, while the Constitution guarantees protection of the freedom of religion, conscientious objectors who object based on religious grounds have had very little attention paid to their rights in this matter.

So it is that persons who identify as conscientious objectors and refuse to serve in the military have put themselves at risk of incarceration for breaching the aforementioned Act of Military Service System. The penalty for such a breach is up to five years in prison (Article 3 of the Punishment Act for Violation to Military Service System).

When a group of convicted conscientious objectors launched an appeal of their conviction to the Judicial Yuan, arguing that it infringed upon their constitutionally protected right to religious freedom, it brought government and societal attention to the issue. While their appeal was rejected by the Council of Grand Justices in 1999, their effort nonetheless bore fruit, leading to an amendment of the Act of Military Service System and the institution of "alternative service" as a non-military option.

Today, the practical reality is that there are a number of ways for conscientious objectors, as well as other young service-age men who simply want to avoid military service, to do so. Successful applicants for the alternative service option have a few possible avenues, including family obligations (such as in the case of a single-parent family, or a demonstrated level of poverty requiring the individual to contribute to the household income) or being a specialist (such as an English specialist, i.e., by producing a university degree from an English-speaking country, or alternatively an English-language teaching certificate issued in Taiwan).

In addition to these "regular" and "specialist" types, there is a third type of alternative service through which a young man may find a job with a company that agrees to act as his sponsor in an alternative service application. His obligation is to remain in that company's employ for a period of three years. Moreover, the draft can be deferred in the pursuit of an advanced degree until the individual reaches the age of 27. Of course, there are also the deferments that can be obtained in cases of physical problems, (mental deficiencies, heart problems, etc.)

It should be noted here that the alternative service system in operation in the ROC was not instituted as a means of dealing with the problem of conscientious objectors — it was a proposal that had been under consideration for years prior, which was fast-tracked into implementation in response to the Judicial Yuan's ruling on the aforementioned appeals case, and to placate social calls for a more equitable system. Nevertheless, priority is given to persons who cite religious or family reasons.

Moreover, the alternative service system serves to provide a channel for conscientious objectors to avoid having to serve in uniform, or to go to prison for their beliefs. As such, it is sometimes considered as a factor in the ROC's designation as a postmodern military (Chen, 2009, p. 92).

Survey results show that Taiwan citizens are overwhelmingly against conscientious objection, with 55.3 percent believing all young men should serve (**Figure 4.2**). That number rises to 73.7 percent when one factors in approval of alternative service channels. Looked at in more detail, it

Figure 4.2. Preferred Conscientious Objection Policy.

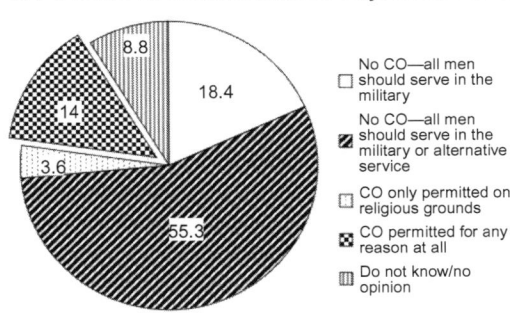

seems that the younger a respondent is, the more likely they are to support conscientious objection. Moreover, the more supportive a respondent is to women serving in the military, the more they support conscientious objection. Taken together, this would seem to indicate that citizens, especially young people, regard the matter of military service as a choice, that should be made by the individual in question – either male or female. This is not the same as opposing conscription, it should be clarified, but that given the fact of conscription, persons with a valid reason for conscientiously objecting should not be forced to serve, or punished if they refuse to do so. This interpretation is bolstered by the simultaneous finding that the vast majority (by a ratio of 3 to 1) want the ROC government to keep conscription. Thus it seems that people recognize a need for conscription, whether as a means to promote good citizenship habits among young men, or because of the China threat, but that opting out of such a system should be accommodated.

In terms of whether respondents would recommend their own children to join the military, Figure 4.3 shows that

Figure 4.3. Willingness to Allow Own Children to Enlist.

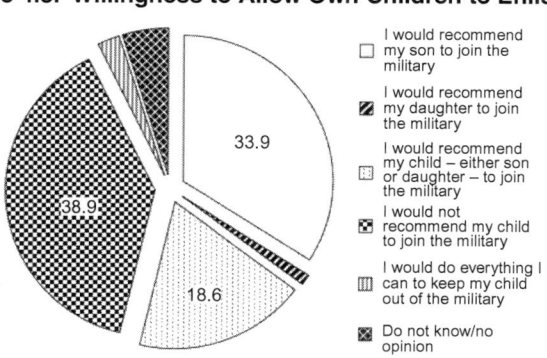

I would recommend my son to join the military

I would recommend my daughter to join the military

I would recommend my child – either son or daughter – to join the military

I would not recommend my child to join the military

I would do everything I can to keep my child out of the military

Do not know/no opinion

almost 40 percent of respondents overall would not recommend that their child — son or daughter — join the military.
When broken down by gender, men are less willing to recommend their child to join up, as are respondents who are less
worried about an attack from China. Likewise, those who
are themselves less willing to fight are less likely to recommend that their children join up. Finally, those who don't
have faith in the military are less willing to recommend that
their child seek military service. While self-identification
has little effect, and attitudes toward one's own children
serving in the military are not impacted significantly by self-
identification, the results obtained are nevertheless instructive. Individuals would seem to view the military as a purely
defensive institution, and not as a possible career path.
Specifically, in the absence of a China threat, there would
seem to be no compelling reason for joining the military.

Interestingly, while attitudes toward one's own children
serving in the military are not impacted by self-identification,
results are different when it comes to oneself. Willingness
to fight was found to be impacted significantly by self-
identification, as can be seen in Figure 4.4. In addition to
youth as a significant factor, the more one identifies as Chinese,
the less willing one is to fight.

This can also be read in the reverse way, that the more
one identifies as Taiwanese, the more willing one is to fight.
This would seem to support similar findings to the effect that
persons who have an ethnic self-identification as Chinese are
significantly less likely to worry about the China threat. In
this case, this worry is put into action, and not only is the
level of worry lower among those self-identifying as Chinese,
but there is less of a willingness to fight as well. This could be
that they simply cannot conceive of such an attack happening
in reality, and hence they have no worry about it and no perceived need to fight, even a hypothetical one. Or it could

Figure 4.4. Willingness to Fight by Ethnic Self-identification.

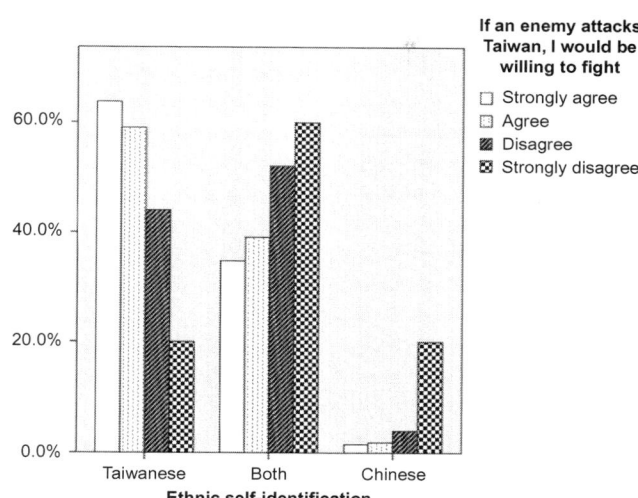

mean that identifying as they do as Chinese, they do not see the PRC as an existential threat, and hence would not take up arms to resist a Chinese annexation of Taiwan.

NOTES

1. This large standing army was made up largely of unskilled, illiterate commoners, many of whom were press-ganged from among the armies of defeated warlords.

2. The Joint Commission on Rural Reconstruction was made up of five commissioners that included three locals selected by the ROC government and two Americans appointed by the US president.

CHAPTER 5

MAJOR MISSION DEFINITION

The changing security environment in East Asia in the post-war years had an enormous impact on the mission definition of the ROC military. Until the defeat of Japan in WWII, in which the ROC was the primary ally in the region, the mission was to win the war in the Pacific. Even afterward, the mission changed little, except that instead of being on a war footing in the attempt to defeat the Japanese, the military was now on a war footing to defeat the People's Liberation Army. Once that conflict resulted in the loss of China to the Communists, and the retreat of the ROC to Taiwan, the military's primary goal then became one of preparing for the launching of an effort to retake the mainland. During the early years of the reign of Chiang Kai-shek, taking back China was the major mission of the ROC military. To that end, soldiers had to be indoctrinated with the party's values, and so troops received instruction in Sun Yassin's Three Principles of the People, and they were fed propaganda on the regime's view of itself as the authentic ruler of China and hence the need to retake the mainland (Edmonds & Tsai, 2006, p. 45).

In its strictest terms, the ROC military defines its mission in a manner that is detailed in the legal canon in accordance with the nation's legislation. Article 137 of the ROC Constitution outlines that "The national defense of the Republic of China shall have, as its objective, the safeguarding of national security and the preservation of world peace" (Taiwan National Security and Defense Law and Regulations Handbook, 2007). Moreover, in Article 2 of Chapter 1 of the National Defense Act, it is stated that "The national defense of the Republic of China aims at utilization of comprehensive national power to establish national defense force, safeguard national security, and maintain world peace." Within this overarching philosophy, mission definition is honed occasionally to ensure its congruence with the political and military realities of the day (Chen, 2009, p. 61).

The first stage of defense was marked by an alignment of ROC and US efforts. From a wider geopolitical perspective, for most of the twentieth century, the cross-strait conflict has always been one front in the wider Cold War that defined the state of global politics, and as such, the mission definition has always been strongly influenced by the ROC allies in America. The events of the 228 Incident of February, 1947 and the decades-long period of martial law, known as the White Terror, will not be described in great detail in this work, though they are worth mentioning as they defined the condition of state—society relations for most of the early decades of KMT rule over Taiwan, and help to explain how the regime of Generalissimo Chiang Kai-shek could exert such complete control over the economy and the social institutions in order to achieve its developmental aims. By the end of the 228 revolt, at least 10,000 had died, and KMT rulers came to realize that changes would be necessary to placate sharecroppers and avoid a repeat of the Communist uprising that had taken place on mainland China. The lynchpin of these efforts would be land reform, as the tenancy system then in place created friction between landlord and tenant. The KMT government responded with rent reduction, followed by 1951's land sale program and the land-to-the-tiller program in 1953, which contributed to appeasing the peasantry and forestalling support for Communist agitators (Tai, 1974, p. 87).

The United States tried to disabuse Chiang of his plan to use Taiwan as a convenient staging point for an invasion to retake the mainland, and President Harry Truman withdrew support for the KMT regime in order to allow State Department and CIA predictions of a communist victory over Chiang's forces on Taiwan to be realized (Christensen, 1996, p. 107). When war broke out in Korea in June 1950, US support for the KMT's and other anti-Communist efforts gained renewed fervor in Washington, and Chiang was once again seen as an ally in the struggle against Communist expansion.

A large part of this alliance consisted of a foreign aid initiative conducted along multiple fronts (economic, as well as military) that would prove to be America's most successful post-war reconstruction effort, rivaling even US efforts in Germany and Japan in terms of efficiency and speed. Conditions in post-war Taiwan were, like those in South Korea, amenable to strong state intervention in economic development and the successful adoption of the developmental state model. These conditions include the presence of a bureaucratic tradition able to implement policy; a power vacuum created by the elimination, by the recent war, of the State's previous power elite (i.e., the Japanese); the existence of unresolved security threats; a cultural commitment to the bourgeois legal order; and belief in the concept of private ownership of property (Woo-Cumings, 1998, p. 336).

In late 1954, America's role as the ROC's security guarantor allowed the KMT regime to reduce military expenditures, and contributed to two decades of relative stability in the Taiwan Strait (Rubinstein, 2013, p. 31). The US role in safeguarding Taiwan's security has allowed for a steady decline of military spending as a share of total government expenditures, dropping from over 40 percent in the 1960s to about 11 percent today (Templeman et al., 2015, p. 4).

During this stage of joint defense with the Americans, the mission of the ROC military remained the recovery of the mainland, in addition to that pronounced in the Constitution and National Defense Act. Despite US distaste for this goal, Chiang Kai-shek held resolutely to returning to rule China, almost to the end. It was only in the 1970s that Chiang came to the realization that any return to China by the ROC would be "70 percent political, 30 percent military" (Guy, 2005, p. 9).

By the 1980s and 1990s, the ROC government had abandoned its dream of retaking the mainland and instead concentrated its efforts on effecting a peaceful unification of the two sides. In contrast, China still has yet to renounce the use of force to annex the island, and continues to threaten military – and exert political and economic – pressure to achieve that end. Today, the strategy in Taipei can best be described as an attempt to maintain the status quo of de facto independence for as long as is possible.

The 1970s to the 1990s was a period of great change in trilateral relations, and hence in the nature of the mission of the ROC military. Normalization of Sino-US relations, termination of the defense treaty, derecognition of Taiwan, and the enactment of the Taiwan Relations Act all had an enormous impact on the defense structure of the island. The mission shifted from one largely, if increasingly half-heartedly, focused on offense in terms of an invasion and retaking of the mainland to one predicated upon defense of the island against Chinese attack. For one thing, US arms sales as promulgated by the TRA were restricted to defensive systems only, and US assistance in the event of invasion was likewise conditioned upon there having been no outright declaration of independence on the part of Taipei as the instigator of said attack (H.R. 2479, 1979). The purpose behind these conditions was to ensure that the political future of the Taiwan Strait be decided peacefully. The proposal by Chiang Ching-kuo, who succeeded his father as ROC President in 1978, that China be unified under Sun Yat-sen's Three Principles of the People was in alignment with a similar proclamation by China's paramount leader, Deng Xiaoping.

As this phase progressed, there were changes taking place in Taiwan culture and politics. In addition to engineering a tentative opening to China, primarily by allowing people from Taiwan to visit family members across the strait, Chiang Ching-kuo initiated an end to martial law. According to a popular way of telling the story, he was on his deathbed, and did not want to die a dictator. Moreover, the ameliorating economy had created a thriving middle class, and thus an increasingly active civil society, pushing for more and greater freedoms (Hsiao, 2014, p. 219). No longer did Taiwanese have to emigrate to the West in order to build a better life for their families; they were building one in Taiwan. Nevertheless, Taiwan was losing the diplomatic war with China on the international stage, and fewer and fewer nations recognized the ROC, with more switching recognition to the PRC every year.

During this period there were two institutional changes, both taking place in 1991, that contributed to a shift in the military mission definition: one was President Lee Teng-hui's promulgation of the Guidelines for National Unification, and the other was the scrapping of the "Temporary Provisions Effective During the Period of Communist Rebellion." This latter represented the disappearance of the final vestiges of martial law under which the KMT ruled the island since 1949. Thus, in the early 1990s, it appeared as though the two sides of the Taiwan Strait were inevitably drifting together, for once peacefully and through a political solution. With the reduced military threat, the mission definition shifted from one of offense to one of defense.

Throughout this period, in addition to growing social and economic freedoms, and amid the loss of diplomatic allies to the PRC, there was a concerted effort to shift the political system to something more democratic. With the US recognition of China in 1979, and the fall of European communism 10 years later, it was clear that anti-communism was no longer a sufficient basis on which to build a common cause with the nations of the West. Thus, democratization served as an ideal way to highlight the shared values between Taiwan and the West, and to position Taiwan as a more acceptable member of the international community than China. Arguably the culmination of these efforts toward democratization was the holding of free and direct presidential elections in 1996. This period, however, coincided with – and exacerbated – a downturn in Taipei–Beijing relations that started with President Lee's visit to his US alma mater, Cornell University. Beijing was incensed that Lee was accepted as though he were the president of a country in its own right, as the PRC still considered Taiwan a renegade province.

To signal its displeasure with the elections being held in Taiwan, as well as to pressure the population to not vote for Lee, the PLA launched missiles into the Taiwan Strait, ostensibly as a military exercise. The activity had the opposite effect, boosting Lee's popularity and helping voter turnout

reach 76 percent, with Lee winning a majority with 54 percent of the votes cast. To dissuade any more aggressive moves
by China, Washington dispatched two aircraft carrier groups
to the region, and the incident came to be known as the
Third Taiwan Strait Crisis.

Thus, during the Lee era, the ROC military stance was
defined by the term "effective deterrence, resolute defense,"
with a focus on the defense of Taiwan proper, while the
offshore islands were more or less relegated to being self-
sufficient should they come under attack, without reliance on
reinforcements (Ministry of Defense, Taiwan, 1996, p. 54).

With the election of a DPP president, Chen Shui-bian, in
2000, a shift occurred in the interpretation of the "effective
deterrence, resolute defense" strategy, calling for an element
of "offensive defense," which translated to a willingness to
deploy air and naval assets to deliver a counterstrike to
command-and-control facilities on the mainland proper,
rather than restricting defensive efforts to close-in defense
against the PLA achieving a beachhead. The concept of
"all-out defense" also gained currency in this era; a term and
policy which exhorted all citizens to take part in the nation's
defense. This policy had the added benefit – as seen through
the eyes of the more independence-minded politicians – of
highlighting the threat from China in the minds of the populace, and tamping the desire for unification with an aggressive
China (Chen, 2009b, p. 10). In contrast, during the Ma
administration that succeeded the Chen years, the mission of
the ROC armed forces began shifting toward a focus on
search and rescue (SAR) and HA/DR, even to the point that
combat readiness became jeopardized. There were two reasons for this: one was the desire to avoid antagonizing China,
and the second was to increase public satisfaction with the
military by showcasing soldiers in high-profile rescue and
humanitarian missions.

In *The Soldier and the Citizen: The Role of the Military in Taiwan's Development*, Monte R. Bullard argues that the ROC military played such an important role in the country's social, political, and economic changes that simplistic civilian control models derived from the literature on civil—military relations are insufficient. Bullard (1997, p. 5) also points out that the threat faced by the ROC military was a two-pronged one: there was the external threat of invasion from China, of course; but in addition, there was the domestic threat posed by independence forces within Taiwan itself. Given that the ROC colonization of Taiwan was unlike colonization in the conventional sense because of the loss of the homeland, forces advocating for Taiwan independence amounted to a greater threat than mere secession or loss of a colony: Taiwan independence would equate to the annihilation of the ROC itself.

5.1. PUBLIC PERCEPTION OF MISSION

The vast majority of Taiwan citizens see the role of the military as one of defense, although those with parents from the mainland tend to think the army's role is to defend "against another country," not necessarily from China per se. As discussed in the previous chapter, the difference between identifying the name of the enemy and not doing so is of little practical difference, and would not affect policy so much as serve as a semantic distinction to make members of a certain group more comfortable with their selection. However, in the search to build a stronger society—military relationship, it is important that the institution of the armed forces adopt a clear identity, and therefore a clear position in society. The inability to articulate the name of the enemy is at odds with the military's role to unambiguously defend the nation against external threats. Moreover, the close ties that have developed in recent years between the KMT and the CCP, coupled with the preponderance of old-guard thinking within the military, threaten to muddy the waters and cause the general population to see the military as an anachronistic, out-of-touch institution that is not in tune with the realities of the threat facing Taiwan. This would have detrimental effects on recruitment, retention, and morale within the military, and with its place in society.

CHAPTER 6

DOMINANT MILITARY PROFESSIONAL AND CIVILIAN EMPLOYEES

6.1. DOMINANT MILITARY PROFESSIONAL IN THE ROC MILITARY

While the National Defense University does an excellent job of producing highly educated and proficient leaders with a strong grounding in the study of combat, Taiwan is not yet at the postmodern stage in this dimension, that of having the dominant military professional be soldier—statesmen and scholar—soldiers. Rather, they are very competent technicians and managers, consistent with a placement in the late modern category. The main reason for this, of course, is external factors affecting the experience obtained by Taiwan's military leaders. Due to the lack of diplomatic allies and the international pressure exerted by China to keep Taiwan from participating in international fora and events, members of the military have not had the opportunity to take part in multinational combat or peacekeeping missions, and the decades-long standoff with China has largely been akin to a Cold

War, with no flare-ups or exchanges of gunfire in at least two generations. As a result, there are few officers with actual combat experience that could be labeled as "combat leaders," and the aforementioned diplomatic blockade makes the acquisition of the relevant experience necessary in becoming a soldier—statesmen all but impossible to Taiwan's officers.

The dominant military professional in the ROC military has traditionally been those officers educated under the military system in Taiwan. In the immediate post-Chinese Civil War years, these professionals tended to be combat leaders: those who had experienced fighting the Japanese and then the Chinese Communists. Since the ROC retreat and entrenchment in Taiwan, with the exception of covert incursions, and early skirmishes with China over the outlying islands, very few military officers obtained direct combat experience, and thus those individuals who received promotion to higher levels of authority and rank were those who received the proper military education. This education was and still is provided by the country's military academies, including the Naval Academy, the Air Force Academy, and the ROC Military Academy founded in the 1950s. At higher levels, officers attended the ROC National Defense University where they received instruction in military strategy at the university's Command and Staff colleges and the War College, provided they passed the rigorous entrance examinations.

In this way, promotion and advancement in the military system is not unlike advancement in the civilian world, wherein students compete with others in their cohort for positions in the nation's high schools, or universities, or civil service, based almost solely on their performance in entrance examinations. It is a system that dates back to the Imperial examination system that was employed to select officials for the civil service, ostensibly on the basis of merit. While the system finds its roots as long ago as the Han dynasty

(221–207 BC), it became the standard in the Tang dynasty (618–907 AD), and it continues to hold sway in Sinophonic cultures to this day.

The main purpose of the advanced military education system in Taiwan is to provide commanding officers with a thorough knowledge of war tactics and prepare them to perform joint military operations. Those officers in line for promotion to the rank of colonel or major general must complete this training, whose curriculum includes such topics as "Military Force Construction," "National Security," "Enemy Research," "International Relations," "War Theory," and "National Defense Decision Making and Management" (Tung, Huang, Keh, & Wai, 2009, p. 490).

Thus, for most of the post-war era and well into the democratization period, military professionals in the ROC received an education that focused on military tactics and values, even as these same officers were barred from accumulating deployment experience due to Taiwan's unique geopolitical isolation. It is important to note at this juncture that the importance and the role of the ROC military went beyond warfighting: it serves as a force for social cohesion in the immediate aftermath of the 1949 retreat to Taiwan and in the years of the greatest threat from the Chinese communists, who themselves were operating as a Bolshevik Organizational Weapon, as described by Selznick (1960). Thus, as a counter to this effort (and indeed, perhaps inspired by it), the ROC military was heavily involved in national integration and political socialization (Bullard, 1997, p. 4), as evidenced by the military's General Political Warfare Department having outright control of the Chinese Television System (CTS).

Thus, the values-oriented aspect of military training, as well as the political indoctrination, was aimed not only at future flag officers with great influence over the nation's

armed forces personnel, but also at those with a great potential influence and responsibility in building the ROC society
on Taiwan. With the coming into force of the National
Defense Organization Act in 2002, which was passed in
part to reorganize ROC defense institutions in such a way
that they could better communicate and cooperate with the
United States military, there followed a rise in the prevalence
of "defense officials" (Chen, 2009, p. 71). As such, the dominant military professional shifted from the type described,
that is, that of a leader educated in combat tactics, to one
that was more managerial in nature.

While many have hailed the civilianization of control over
the ROC military in the early 2000s as the most important
evolution thus far undertaken by the ROC military, it has
not been without its problems. Prior to the aforementioned
legislation, there were just 28 civilians among the Defense
Ministry's 224-strong personnel. While that number reached
167 by late 2004, it became difficult to find enough non-
military personnel with an expertise in security analysis and
defense affairs. Moreover, in addition to there being problems with the Defense Minister and Vice Minister being
allowed to appoint civilian officials to middle-management
posts, in many cases, the ostensibly civilian officials taking up
many of the posts — including in the early days, the post of
Minister of National Defense — have been career military officers who had recently retired (Chase, 2006, p. 4). Therefore,
it is difficult to ascertain just how effective the shift to civilian
control has been, and how much is merely to make it look
good on paper. The ROC military is not yet at the postmodern stage wherein the dominant military professional is the
scholar—soldier, however, there are indications that events
are heading in that direction. Established in 2000 to replace
the Armed Forces University, the ROC National Defense

University offers advanced degrees in a variety of advanced fields.

It should be noted that there is an ethnic component to the question of military officials, at least in terms of who received advancement and promotions and who does not. The time-line for many of the force restructuring discussed previously was during the democratic era, and more specifically, during the DPP administration of President Chen Shui-bian. This was happening as two pieces of legislation went into effect in 2002: the National Defense Law and the Organization Law of the MND. Through them, the military would be headed by a civilian, the cabinet-level post of defense minister, and one-third of Defense Ministry positions were to be staffed by civilians (Edmonds & Tsai, 2006, p. 45). Prior to the 2000 elections in which the KMT lost power in Taiwan for the first time in 55 years, high-ranking officers in the ROC military were, as a general rule, made up of ethnic Mainlanders – Taiwanese officers simply did not receive promotions. Writing in the early 1960s, Axelbank (1963) noted that in the 600,000-strong military of the day, Taiwanese made up more than 75 percent of the ground troops, while the number of Taiwanese officers above the rank of colonel could be counted on both hands, despite the fact that there were nearly 1,000 generals and admirals.

It was this practice of selective promotions that led to the distrust that Chen Shui-bian had in the armed forces, consid-ering the military a threat to the cause of independence, or even localization. Indeed, after winning the presidency in 2000, many pundits were speculating on the likelihood of a military coup to prevent the DPP forces from taking power. Chen nevertheless made successful efforts, first in placating the military – accomplished largely by choosing as his first Premier Tang Fei, a highly respected former Air Force general – and second in shifting the ethnic imbalance among flag officers. This was accomplished by opening up the higher ranks to ethnic Taiwanese and holding promotions every six months (instead of the previous 12) in order to expedite the staffing of flag officer positions with Taiwanese. By the end of his first term in office, Chen had reportedly changed three-quarters of the nation's generals. Moreover, the president would dispatch DPP legislators and local politicians to pay a friendly visit to the homes and offices of high-ranking military officers to surreptitiously check whether they had portraits of the DPP president hanging prominently in both places, thus attesting to their loyalty (Su, 2009, p. 272).

6.2. PUBLIC PERCEPTION OF DOMINANT MILITARY PROFESSIONAL

Given this history of animosity between the ROC military's traditional role and the trend toward localization, it is little wonder that people are concerned about confusion in national identity, especially regarding how it impacts the military. There is an across-the-board consensus that the main problem facing today's ROC military is confusion about national identity, with 38.1 percent of respondents choosing this option to best represent their belief about where the problem lies (see Figure 6.1).

It should be noted that the next-highest option, at 30.5 percent, was "outdated attitudes within the military." Survey results show that men, blue voters, and respondents with both identities (Chinese and Taiwanese) are more worried (though only slightly) about confusion in national identity than are women, green voters, and those who identify as Taiwanese. This dimension has a far-reaching impact on issues other than personnel, but if it is the individuals that make up an organization who are responsible for contributing to the identity of

Figure 6.1. Main Problem Facing the Military.

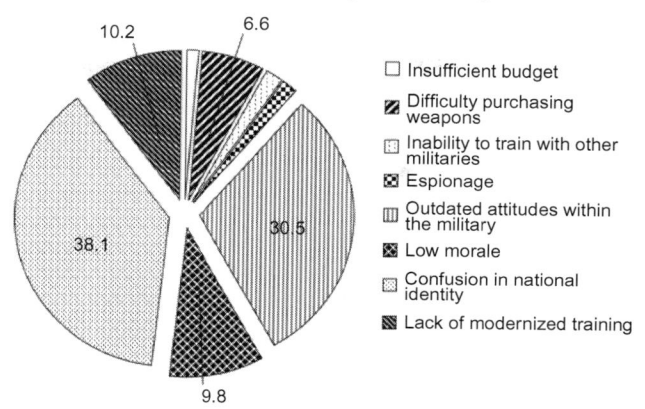

10.2   6.6

□ Insufficient budget

▨ Difficulty purchasing weapons

▦ Inability to train with other militaries

⊠ Espionage

▥ Outdated attitudes within the military

▨ Low morale

▨ Confusion in national identity

◨ Lack of modernized training

38.1   30.5

9.8

that organization, then personnel changes might be a most efficient way for military planners to solve these problems and make the military more responsive to the general population, and a more appropriate social institution in today's Taiwan.

6.3. CIVILIAN EMPLOYEES IN THE ROC MILITARY

While there is a medium component of civilian employees working alongside members of the ROC military, which is consistent with the late modern model, there are some unique characteristics behind the numbers that paint a picture of a very different situation than the one experienced by western militaries and on which the PMMM is based. As described, the civilian employees in the ROC military appear to be concentrated at the high end and the low end: assisting in planning and decision-making, as well as performing as soldier-type employees. There is a much lower degree of civilians who — either because they possess technical skills unavailable to the service member, or because they can perform menial tasks cheaper than the ROC soldier (an unlikely prospect in a system with conscription) — are integrated in an operational role at ROC military bases and vessels. Thus, the penetration of civilian employees into the operational side of military operations is a minor component, and this dimension is most closely aligned with the modern era.

Until Taiwan's democratization, the degree of civilian employment in the armed forces was negligible. Those that did operate in conjunction with serving members were very much divided along the same lines as officers and men, with two types of civilian contractors: officer-type and soldier-type. Like their commissioned counterparts, the officer-type had classified clearance, and were primarily made up of retired officers. The soldier-type had usually females hired to perform duties akin to their counterparts in the civilian job market: office girls who, in this case, were restricted to handling accounting, processing nonclassified documents, and performing similar clerical tasks. In terms of numbers, these soldier-type civilian employees far outnumbered those of the officer-type. Presumably, the gender wage gap that existed in Taiwan at that time made this an attractive option to the military, as well as civilian, hiring managers of the day. In other words, while it may have appeared on paper that the military employed civilian workers, in practice this was very different from the intent as described by Moskos's model (Chen, 2009, p. 82).

Beginning in the 1980s, force downsizing plans (i.e., the Force Reorganization Project of 1992—1995, and the Ten-Year Force Structure Project of 1993—2003) saw the number of civilian employees decrease even further as their tasks were delegated to serving members. The ease with which civilian employees could be laid off was accomplished by their being held to military employment standards, and not the stipulations of labor law that governed employer—employee relations in the civilian world. Thus, in times of fiscal difficulty, they were the first to go, not least because as civilians their role was seen by military members as being less important than that of persons in uniform. This perception lasted until well into the 2000s.

To some degree, 2002's National Defense Act and National Defense Organization Act ameliorated this situation, especially in terms of their numbers. According to the 2004 National Defense Report of the Republic of China (Taiwan), the ratio of civilian employees to uniformed officers and men jumped from 12.5 percent prior to implementation of the aforementioned legislation to 29.3 percent just two years afterward. Moreover, there has been a qualitative improvement in civilian participation as well, with non-uniformed employees contributing to the decision-making and planning processes. This is also reflected in the higher average level of education of civilian employees: whereas many of the aforementioned soldier-type employees prior to democratization had a high-school education, by 2004, 36.1 percent of civilian employees held advanced degrees, with most of the remaining having bachelor degrees (Chen, 2009, p. 83). Thus, the pattern of civilian employees in the ROC military appears to be concentrated at the high end and the low end – the high end being the planning and decision-making within the defense organization, and the low end consisting of clerks and other soldier-type employees. Even though, by numbers, they would appear to be a medium component of the ROC's military, the nature of their role is inconsistent with the integration of civilians on the operational side of the defense establishment. These include the civilian technicians, or tech reps, that are stationed at air bases and ships of the US military because they have technical skills and training unavailable to the service member, or the civilians contracted to perform menial tasks and thereby release more active service members for training and deployment. In both cases, the ROC military's limited budget makes service members a more viable option, keeping the penetration of civilian employees into the operational side of military operations down to a minor component, and hence keeping this dimension at the modern era.

CHAPTER 7

SPOUSES AND THE MILITARY COMMUNITY

The ROC military is consistent with the postmodern military in terms of spouses and the role they play in the military experience. In effect, the spouses have been removed from military life today, with very little overlap between the worlds of family and military.

When looking at the changing roles that husbands and wives respectively play in a marriage in Taiwan, the influence of Confucianism and what it has to say about filial piety and the father–son dyad must be taken into account. The kinship system is dominated by the father–son dyad in Chinese culture, as opposed to the husband–wife dyad that dominates in western cultures. The dominant attributes of the father–son dyad include continuity, inclusiveness, authoritativeness, and asexuality. For example, the father–son dyad emphasizes the continuity of the family name, linear authoritative relations among family members, extended households, collective benefits for the family, and each family member's role and responsibilities. In contrast, the husband–wife dyad stresses equality of the sexes, affectionate bonds between the husband and wife, nuclear households, and the well-being of individuals (Hsu, 1971, p. 18).

Among the factors influencing family ideology, younger age, higher education, and an urban background are all consistently found to be influential to modern ideologies (Hochschild & Machung, 1989; Tsai & Yi, 1987). For example, younger married couples (aged 20–39) and metropolitan families tend to prefer nuclear households, while their older and less urbanized counterparts do not. Meanwhile, regardless of age, people who have more education are more likely to prefer nuclear households (Freedman, Thornton, & Yang, 1994). In addition, couples living in urban areas are often more likely to make joint family decisions (Yi & Lu, 1996). As a result, an assumption may be made that the more industrialized and modern Taiwan's society becomes, the further the family power structure moves away from the traditional father–son dyad and toward a more western-style husband–wife dyad.

In addition, we may further deduce that a modern husband–wife dyad is representative of an improvement in women's status in the family. Thus, for this dimension, we will look at the changing status of married women in Taiwan, focusing on three factors representative of the husband–wife dyad. These three factors are education, employment, and family structure.

Much research has concluded that individuals with higher levels of education tend to have a more egalitarian view of gender status and believe in interchangeable gender roles in the family. A majority of modernization theorists believe that higher education is the most important factor in improving the status of women. As a result, highly educated couples are often associated with the improved status of women in the family. Despite criticisms concerning gender stereotypes, the levels of inequality between men and women in terms of education in Taiwan are decreasing. As such, indirect positive effects for women's status in the family may be deduced as well (Chang, 1994, p. 7).

It is commonly accepted that, since the post-war period, Taiwan's educational system has improved substantially with regard to the equality of men and women. In 1995, the percentage of female students at all educational levels was close to half of all students, or close to a 1:1 student sex ratio. Several factors are often attributed to the improved access to education for women over the last few decades. These factors include economic growth, smaller family sizes, public education up to senior high school, and the changing attitudes of parents and women.

Nonetheless, statistics also reveal that as educational levels advance, the disparity between men and women continues. In rural areas of Taiwan, the patrilineal belief is still existent and continues to influence family decisions about education. In short, sons normally enjoy a higher priority than daughters in family resource allocation. Thus, despite improved educational opportunities for women, social and cultural factors continue to perpetuate differences in the type and quality of education received by men and women in Taiwan.

An important indicator of marital status is the number of resources each spouse brings to the union. Economic resources, involving income, status, and prestige based on success in the professional world, are arguably the most important of family resources. Today, most women in Taiwan view themselves as holding a better position in the family and in society than previous generations. Younger women who are well educated and living in urban areas have a modern outlook on life and enjoy a degree of independence that was not possible for their mothers born in the 1960s. Studies have shown that professional women exert more

influence on the family decision-making process than women
with nonprofessional jobs, especially in the management of
household finances (Yi & Chang, 1995).

It is widely accepted that women played an important role
throughout Taiwan's economic development. As for married
women, their role increased during the development of light
industry in Taiwan. During this time, married women nearing
the end of child-bearing age began to reenter the workforce,
making up for a decrease in the availability of young female
workers due to declining fertility rates and increased household expenses (Lu, 2000). Meanwhile, during the 1980s, the
role of women in the labor force began to shift from cheap,
semi-skilled labor to skilled labor. In 1982, for the first time,
white-collar employment opportunities exceeded blue-collar
employment opportunities for women, and women's participation in the tertiary sector (retail businesses, social services,
insurance, and commerce) has since grown (DGBAS, 1996).

With the female labor force expanding considerably since
1970 due to a need for unskilled labor, increases in urban
tertiary employment, a rise in women's educational levels,
and the trend toward smaller families, the status of women in
the family has improved. Nonetheless, when looking at the
increased burden for married women, inequalities are still evident. Even today, women continue to carry the extra burden
of household responsibilities in spite of advancement in the
workplace. At home, women remain responsible for household tasks, maintaining the family's finances and looking
after elderly parents-in-law. As a result, despite the achievements of married women in the workforce, the problem of
balancing work and family continues to be ever-present
today. Due mainly to a lack of acceptable low-cost elderly-
care facilities, along with traditional attitudes concerning
child — parent relations, the rule of Confucian filial piety
to respect and support elderly parents is still prevalent in

Taiwan society. In addition, financial and nonfinancial assistance provided by parents continue to consolidate intergenerational ties.

In summary, family ideology in Taiwan continues to be in transition from the traditional father – son dyad toward the modern husband – wife dyad. It appears that advances in family ideology are not modernizing at the same rate. Kinship ideology with respect to intergenerational relations is lagging behind gender ideology with respect to marital relations. For intergenerational relations, patrilineal ideology is persistent in Taiwan. Sons continue to be obligated to take care of older parents. Nonetheless, studies have shown that education and level of income, as well as the rise of individualistic values, are gradually eroding the authority of parents. In marital relations, gender status has evolved faster than gender roles. Meanwhile, egalitarianism and specialized roles for husbands and wives are dominant norms today.

How does this society-wide trend affect the role that spouses play in the military life? Little work has been done on studying this issue in Taiwan, although a few studies have touched upon the place of family in a successful military career. In the immediate post-war period, the issue of spouses and families was one that was strictly institutionally controlled, at least in the lives of rank-and-file soldiers. Soldiers were forbidden to marry in the late 1940s and early 1950s, with the reason cited for this being the national effort to retake the mainland. Presumably, it was feared that the psychological effect of "settling down" in Taiwan would dampen the soldiers' zeal to leave the island in order to recapture the Chinese homeland from the Communists. This policy was relaxed somewhat in the mid-1950s, but marriage was still strictly controlled: soldiers could submit to their superiors an application for marriage, accompanied by a medical report on both parties (Chen, 2009, p. 89).

It was much easier in this era for officers to marry, and in fact, marriages followed the pattern described by Moskos et al. of an institutional arrangement, with spouses playing an integral role to the military life. Starting in the 1950s, the National Women's League — an organization made up mostly of officers' wives — contributed to the overall military effort and the upkeep of morale by running charity drives, sewing uniforms, caring for injured servicemen, and providing classes. The group was founded in 1950 by the wife of Chiang Kai-shek, Soong Mei-ling, and its membership primarily consisted of the wives of high-ranking officers. As such, it has often been considered a subsidiary of the KMT. Over the years, the group has raised billions of dollars in its fundraising efforts, and had a demonstrable effect in raising morale. The group's centrality to the military experience declined in the mid-1970s after Chiang's death, and after Madame Chiang left Taiwan to take up residence in the United States, but it continues its work even today, albeit in a less influential form.

Another aspect of the dimension of military spouses in Taiwan is the existence of military dependents' villages. These settlements were designed to integrate the family experience with the military experience. They were originally built for the soldiers from the mainland who retreated with the KMT to Taiwan in 1949. The idea was to isolate these men, and later their families, from the wider society, largely as a means to stave off assimilation. Not surprisingly, a unique subculture was created, one marked by isolation from Taiwanese culture, but wherein the individual cultures from the various and far-flung provinces of the Chinese homeland were represented and, to a degree, preserved.

It is worth noting that the military dependents village subculture was very supportive of the KMT, and served as a symbol of the overall separation between the ROC military and Taiwan society. The villages espoused an ethic of patriotism and hard work, with a premium on self-reliance — even the food was subsidized by the government, meaning that the inhabitants had less cause to shop in the Taiwanese markets. Despite the fact that many of the soldiers' wives were Taiwanese, they followed the traditional Chinese custom of deferring to the husband as the head of the household, and the wife as leaving her family to join that of her husband. In later years, as the mainland soldiers began to retire, the villages continued on, and they formed an ideal incubator for officer corps candidates in subsequent generations, in the form of the sons who grew up in these pro-KMT, pro-military, isolated environments. In essence, they represent an extreme example of an institutional military (according to Moskos's I/O concept) wherein all the good things in life are provided to the soldier by his military superiors. They go beyond this, in fact, creating a subculture that identifies with the military and the party, down through the generations.

The subculture incubated in the dependents' villages, as well as other military-first forces such as the Women's League, began to decline in the 1980s and 1990s as the third generation of this subculture began to yearn for different lives and opportunities than those available to their parents. Officers began to marry at younger ages, for example, and regulations governing approval for marriage were overhauled in 1992: applications still had to be submitted, but if no response was received within 30 days, the individual was free to proceed with the wedding. This simple fact constituted a release of the psychological grip that the military institution had on its members. Likewise, the Women's League shifted its focus and took on a broader range of societal activities, even as its membership declined among the younger generation.

By the 1990s, the villages themselves underwent physical and administrative reconstruction that essentially ended their pro-KMT, pro-military incubation function. The government began to eye alternative uses for the land on which the villages were situated, and alternative accommodations were made to the mostly lower-income residents while reconstruction work was under way, with the relocations essentially severing the community connections that had been formed among residents. The refurbished villages, moreover, were no longer restricted to being used only by military personnel, becoming instead regular communities that may or may not include some military families among the regular inhabitants. As a result, the military families became integrated with the wider Taiwanese culture to a much greater degree, and began to develop a level of independence from relying on the military and government for their daily existence.

Thus, the three factors which most represented the military's centrality in issues of spouses and family, the dependents villages, the National Women's League, and the marriage requirements, all lost most of their power by the turn of the millennium (Chen, 2009, p. 89). Being largely removed from their previous role in military life, spouses and military families can be categorized as having reached the postmodern stage according to the PMMM.

CHAPTER 8

WOMEN AND THE MILITARY

Women's participation in the military, while officially unfet-tered by any legalistic obstacles to full participation, can still best be described as partial integration, again putting Taiwan in the late modern stage.

8.1. FEMINIST PERSPECTIVE OF WOMEN'S ROLE IN THE MILITARY

The traditional view posits two more or less opposing feminist perspectives on the subject of women serving in the military. Those who espouse a fundamentally anti-military worldview oppose all forms of militarism as they see it as part of the cause (along with the "patriarchy" in general) of women having been forced into a position of second-class citizenship in society. In opposition to this view, feminist soldiers see military service as their right, and equally with their male counterparts, their responsibility toward earning first-class citizenship. Generally, those espousing these two perspectives do not engage with one another (Feinman, 2000, p. 89).

Today, the question of military and gender is far more nuanced, not just due to evolution in feminist perspectives, but on the role of the military. For one thing, the post-9/11 conflicts in which the United States and many forces from the western world are engaged are fundamentally different from the traditional view of how combat is conducted. Fighting in counterinsurgency operations is conducted by necessity in a way that the concept of being on the "front line" is not so well-defined as it once was, and thus the risks incurred by combat specialists and those by advance support trades may not be that different in practice, and thus exclusion of women from combat roles and their inclusion in support roles lacks the distinction it once had.

In addition to the increased complexities on the field of battle, the motivating factors behind women's inclusion in the armed forces are likewise more complex, demanding a more nuanced position on the part of feminist perspectives on the topic. As has already been covered, the transition that many western militaries made during the decade of the 1990s to a PMMM involved significant sea changes to the land-scape, primarily in terms of increased professionalization, diversification, increased civilian integration, and type of military professional. In addition to the abolishment of conscription and the AVF transition, these changes led to a demand for the type of specialists ideally suited to female participation from the perspective of equality between male and female individuals (Stachowitsch, 2012, p. 305).

Since the 1990s, however, the nature of the conflicts the West has been engaged in has led to the rise of a new para-digm wherein, rather than embracing gender neutrality, the participation of women has been sought specifically because of the perceived differences of the sexes. Specifically, the participation of women in uniform and the apparent dismantling of traditional gender roles became, in itself, an indicator of the superiority of the western model over the enemy; to wit: the Taliban and other Islamic fundamentalist forces that truly treated women as second-class citizens. denying them an education; using gang rape as a punishment for adultery; forbidding them from congregating with men outside the family, etc.

Thus, traditional perspectives on the qualities of femininity, and especially their differences with masculinity, were not sought to be erased, but rather highlighted, in order to demonstrate western concepts of equality and win the hearts and minds of populations in Iraq, Afghanistan, and throughout the Middle East. In practice, Female Engagement Teams were deployed strategically, to build bridges with the local society and collect human intelligence, according to population-centric counterinsurgency theory (Dyvik, 2013, p. 410). The image of women as peacemakers rather than warriors was leveraged, harking a return to the traditional female role in common perception, and a retreat from the concept of gender equality, largely for the purpose of illustrating the cultural sensitivity, and hence superiority, of western society and all that it sought to bring to the Middle East in an effort to stabilize the region: that is, democracy, equality, and liberal society (Stachowitsch, 2012, p. 312).

The feminist perspective on this phenomenon has been largely unified in the view that it is a retreat from wider gains made in the push for gender equality. It capitalizes on a fundamental view of women as the weaker sex, and posits the superiority of western culture because it nonetheless includes them. Moreover, it dismisses individual agency and treats women as a unified cadre with common interests and goals, as opposed to individuals (Shepherd, 2008, p. 27).

The western military and its experience with gender integration has, in recent years, led to a more complex response from feminist thinkers, as well as an end to the previous duality between the integrationist position of equality ethicists and the anti-militarist position of peace ethicists (Stachowitsch, 2012, p. 308).

8.2. ROLE OF WOMEN IN CHINESE CULTURE

It is perhaps not surprising that militaries, being the change-averse institutions that they tend to be, do not lead the wider society in participation by women, but rather follow. Taiwan is no exception, although for such a traditional society, the advancements made by women in Taiwan have been rapid and impressive. Unlike in the West, women in Taiwan did not join the workforce until relatively recently. In traditional Chinese societies, women are considered – at least on the surface – as housebound, second-class citizens whose value lies in obedience first to fathers, then husbands, and finally sons.

Although the early Chinese had no real commitment to the subordination of women, as Confucian teachings spread far and wide and were expanded upon through time, the subordination of women evolved as a common characteristic of all Confucian societies. It was during the Han dynasty (206 BC–220 AD) that Confucianism was adopted as state doctrine, with Confucius's writing becoming an integral component of official education.

An egalitarian society does not have barriers that keep its members apart: a hierarchically Confucian one does. Forces for division exist, and to understand them at the ideological level, Confucianism appeals to the family model. Two facts central to the model are biological inequality and the need for cooperation. Within the family context, the strong help the weak and the weak offer their services and respect. Thus, the king rules his subjects, the parents rule their children, the husband rules his wife, the older brother rules his younger siblings, and so on. According to the Confucian ideal, there is no fear of this power being abused because the strong are tempered by natural affection (Tuan, 1982, p. 25). This intellectual and ethical tradition finds human beings arranged within a natural order. Society is not created but is an outcome of existence. The roles of men and women are thus clearly established by nature itself. The destiny of the individual is inseparable from the personal fulfillment attained through facing the immediate needs and responsibilities of human life (DeBary, 1969, p. 126).

With the Chinese Nationalists' flight to Taiwan in 1949, Confucianism was seen as a moral defense against the undesirable cultural byproducts of modernization (Harrell & Huang, 1994, p. 5). In Taiwan, neo-Confucian interpretations reinforced male authority and patrilineal customs. According to the Confucian structure of society, women at every level were to occupy positions lower than men. Most Confucians accepted the subservience of women as natural and proper. A woman's honor and power were as mother and mother-in-law within the family structure.

Within Confucian ideology, the gender of a child determines its importance within society and the family. Sons bear the promise of continued lineage, of wealth, and of power. Daughters can only offer, to their families, service and respect and, to society, their ability to produce more men. Within the Confucian paradigm, a woman's power comes through the birth of a son — a son to whom later she must offer the same service and respect that she offered to her father and husband. Only with the birth of a son can a woman shed her nonentity status in the familial lineage and society. Therefore, many women find themselves in the catch-22 of wanting and needing to perpetuate the son preference that leads to the devaluation of women.

Seeking out the only means of greater importance and familial power, women were often desperate to bear sons. A woman was defined by her ability, or lack thereof, to provide a son. Elizabeth Johnson states, "Without sons, a woman's existence was without meaning, and she and her husband had little security in this life or the next" (Rankin, 1975, p. 39). The external and internal pressure for a woman to bear a male child was substantial. Those women who failed to produce a son were often ostracized by their husband's families as well as their own. According to Chen Man-hua, "Committing suicide seemed to be one of the solutions for many of these women [...] from 1920 to 1940 [...] young Taiwan women had the highest suicide rate in the world" (Chen, 1999, pp. 21–22). That women would choose death over life without a son speaks volumes about how much daughters were valued.

In America during WWII, the necessities of the war effort prompted great strides in female participation in the workforce, most famously in manufacturing and other sectors that were traditionally dominated by men, as the men were conscripted into the fight. Likewise, albeit to a lesser degree, women in Taiwan found work in factories during the island's rapid industrialization, compounded by the fact that young men were, like their American counterparts of a generation prior, conscripted into mandatory military service. Likewise, on the issue of access to education, women have made great strides from just a generation ago, perhaps due to the growing number of Taiwanese universities, each in need of a constant stream of matriculating students, coupled with the declining birth rate. In the 30 to 34 age cohort, 89 percent of women had completed high school and 48 percent had completed a four-year university program in 2014. For women in the 55 to 59 age cohort who received their education a generation ago, those numbers are 48 percent and 9 percent, respectively. Indeed, as more young, unmarried women chose to pursue the educational opportunities available to them, industries began to find it difficult to staff the factories, and were forced to break, or at least bend, another social taboo: that of hiring large numbers of married women and mothers (Yu, 2015, p. 3). How did this paradigm shift come about?

8.3. WOMEN IN THE WORKFORCE

During the period in which Taiwan was becoming a modernized nation, shifting from an agricultural to an industrial economy, families experienced new opportunities and economic stresses as the family unit altered from one geared toward production to one primarily of consumption. At the same time, women began to enter the workforce in ever-greater numbers to meet the needs created by these all-encompassing social and economic changes. Conceptions of the role of women in Taiwan began slowly to shift, partly as a result of their contribution to the island's rapid industrial development – a phenomenon known today as the "Taiwan Miracle." The hiring patterns of southern Taiwan's export processing zones typify the industrial demand for female laborers, many of whom moved from farms and poor urban families to find employment and contribute to family income. This accompanied a shift in the conception of the family as a source of pooled labor to a source of pooled wages (Gold, 1996, p. 52). By 1977, 85 percent of the 67,000 direct-labor workers employed by businesses in the three zones were women, most of whom were young and unmarried (Arrigo, 1980, p. 25).

As the island became wealthier, it experienced a rise in the relative importance of the service industry, or tertiary sector. By 1980, employment in the agricultural sector dropped to about 20 percent. During the next five years, this figure dropped to 17.5 percent, while great gains were made in the service sector of the economy (Speare, Liu, & Tsay, 1988, p. 83). Many of the women who found themselves employed in the service industry were hired as sales clerks, or for jobs in beauty salons, electronic manufacturing, and food supply, essentially, positions without authority. Meanwhile, most jobs demanding physical labor in the electronics, steel, construction, and transportation industries went to men. There is another sector of the economy, however, where some women did find themselves in positions of authority, namely, in the island's many small- and medium-sized enterprises (SMEs).

The island's SMEs make up the majority of businesses in Taiwan and contributed greatly to the growth of the economy. Women played an integral role in the establishment and operation of these companies and, by some accounts, constituted the majority of the workforce in Taiwan's SMEs. The reason for this is that they are essentially family businesses. As such, their success was due in large part to a family network, of which Taiwan's women have often been a binding force. As discussed, women in Taiwan have traditionally been responsible for taking care of the domestic and economic affairs of the family. As more and more families engaged in SMEs, that role was expanded to include vital and often leadership roles in these family businesses, working as accountants, cooks, laborers, and bosses (Hu, 2003, p. 1). Indeed, although the nominal heads of most of these businesses were men, it was often the female employees who were fluent in English and other foreign languages and who shouldered a great deal of responsibility, especially in handling correspondence with foreign firms. Many of today's female managers began their careers essentially as secretaries in SMEs (Cheng & Liao, 1993, p. 65).

Along with the rapid development of Taiwan came the rapid growth of individual businesses and of Taiwan-based branches of multinational corporations. Demand for managers increased during the 1970s far faster than qualified men could be hired and trained, thereby applying pressure in favor of promoting or hiring female managers. Still, in order to secure such promotions, many women had to seriously outperform rather than merely match the performance of their male coworkers.

Moreover, there are many professions in areas such as law, computers, and international trade where gender bias is less pronounced and which therefore attract many female applicants. As demand for professionals increased, so did the participation of women, primarily by using their education to make advances. Despite this, women's representation in the managerial ranks is still not on par with that of men. In 1992, for example, women accounted for 42 percent of professionals but only 11 percent of managers (Cheng & Liao, 1993, p. 1). By 2014, that number had risen to a much improved, though still low, 26 percent of women in senior management positions (Brooks, 2014).

The reason for this appears to be a lingering prejudicial attitude toward women in the workplace. This attitude was measured in a pair of surveys conducted in Taipei in 1963 and 1991, which were designed to ascertain the change in men's attitudes toward the idea of equal pay for work of equal value. In 1963, 67.6 percent of respondents agreed that women should be paid on par with men. About 28 percent expressed the belief that women should be paid differently, while 4 percent were undecided. By 1991, the proportion of men who agreed with the principle of equal pay increased slightly to 73.1 percent, while 24.2 percent of men disagreed and just under 4 percent remained undecided (Marsh, 1998, p. 126). These results are interesting for a couple of reasons, the first of which is the apparently large proportion of men — over half — who, at a relatively early stage of Taiwan's development, agreed with the progressive notion of equal pay for work of equal value. The second surprise was the lack of any real change in this attitude despite nearly three decades of progress and development. Indeed, this 28-year period saw significant development in almost every facet of Taiwanese life, including major advances in political democratization, the formation of a civil society, economic development, and wealth creation.

In March 2002, the government passed the Gender Equality Employment Law. This law made sexual harassment and discrimination in the workplace chargeable offenses and allows women to take up to two years of maternity leave. Furthermore, female employees may request a day of menstruation leave every month — to be incorporated into sick leave — due to excessive menstrual discomfort. Under the new law, women — including unmarried women and those with adopted children — may request leave due to miscarriage or to raise children. According to many, the law may be a mixed blessing. Shortly after it was enacted, a KMT think tank called the National Policy Foundation conducted a survey showing that almost 70 percent of Taiwan businesses antici- pate managerial difficulties to arise from the new legislation. Specifically, the executives and human resources managers polled expressed apprehension about the provisions allowing for monthly menstrual leave and two-year maternity leave. Although approximately 68 percent indicated that the new law would not prompt a cut in the number of women on their company's payroll, about 32 percent admitted the provisions of the new law would serve as a general disincentive to hiring more female employees (Taipei Times, March 10, 2002).

Despite this possibility, women's organizations in Taiwan expressed optimism about the new law insofar as they considered it a step in the right direction. There were admittedly problems, but through time and education many hoped that Taiwan would follow the Scandinavian model, wherein leave taken for the birth and caring for a child is not considered solely the responsibility of the mother but that of the father as well. Indeed, the law already allows each male employee to take two days off in paid paternity leave when his wife is in labor. In the future, fathers might opt to take leaves of absence from their work to care for the very young. The reality of economic concerns in the family may indicate that, with wife and husband both employed outside of the home, it would be more beneficial for whichever spouse has a higher salary to remain at work, and the other to stay at home. This is becoming increasingly important as the percentage of Taiwan households in which women are the primary breadwinners is steadily increasing, having reached an all-time high in 2015 with approximately 2.45 million households, or 29.2 percent, being supported primarily by female income earners (Taiwan Today, 2016).

To summarize, it is evident that women have contributed greatly to the economic development of Taiwan and also benefited from it. However, despite the fact that women have had more opportunities for higher education and professional positions, men's attitudes toward women in the workforce seem to have changed little.

8.4. THE WOMEN'S MOVEMENT IN TAIWAN

The women's movement in Taiwan, which began in earnest in the 1980s, concentrated most of its efforts on the issues of equal pay and equal employment opportunities, as well as sharing household responsibilities with men (Marsh, 1998, p. 116). Taiwan's rapid economic and democratic advancement took place at a time when gender issues were an urgent point of issue in the societies Taiwan adopted as its developmental models, for example, America and Japan. As a result, the island's middle class became conscious of the issue of gender equality, and a grassroots movement rose up to restructure old relationship patterns and redefine the role of women. Their efforts thus far have, by and large, been successful, although most feminists would agree there is much work yet to be done.

According to a 1999 study by the Council of Labor Affairs, women are usually employed in nonprofessional positions while men are disproportionately represented in top management jobs. Members of the Awakening Foundation — a Taiwanese women's rights group — agitated in June 1987 for fair employment practices for female employees of the Sun Yet-san Memorial Hall. The management policy required female employees to resign upon turning 30 years old or becoming pregnant, whichever came first. The policy was hardly unique among Taiwan businesses and organizations, but the group's decision to picket a famous national landmark brought instant attention to the call for equality. The foundation and other women's rights groups on the island studied foreign equal-rights legislation and composed the first draft of a gender equality bill in 1989. They met with resistance from the powerful business community, however, and although several versions of the bill were tabled over the years, none passed.

In 2002, the government promulgated the aforementioned Gender Equality Employment Law. Made up of seven chapters and 40 articles, the law included a symbolic declaration that employees of both sexes should be treated equally in terms of employment opportunities, salary, promotion, and assignments. Although the law is imperfect, it demonstrated an understanding on the part of the government and society as a whole that women were no longer to be relegated to the home, and the evolution of women's employment patterns over the long term shows that gender inequality in pay has indeed decreased. Still, in 2014, the gender pay gap was 17.5, based on the OECD method of calculation (the difference between male and female median wages divided by the male median wages, among full-time employees). This is very close to the number for the United States, at 17.9, and far better than those for Japan (26.6) and Korea (36.6) (Yu, 2015, p. 5). While this statistic, using this method of calculation, implies more about women's expanded employment choices than it does about the state of equal pay for work of equal value, it nevertheless paints Taiwan in a relatively advanced light. Although it took longer to see the effects of this advancement in the realm of the ROC military, advancements have indeed been made on that front as well.

8.5. WOMEN IN THE ROC MILITARY

From the 1950s to the early 1990s, there was a separate corps for female volunteers, and the role played by women was mostly restricted to nursing and working in the political warfare department, which dealt primarily with propaganda and ideology, after having respectively graduated from the College National Defense Medical College and Fu Shing Kang College, formerly known as the Political Warfare Cadres Academy. The duties of the latter consisted of promulgating political propaganda, providing psychological assistance, and boosting morale among the troops by organizing arts performances. Despite having a separate corps for female members, they existed within a chain of command that included no female flag officers, and any lateral move to the combat branches of the services was restricted (Chen, 2009, p. 83).

With Taiwan's democratization came the opening of a few military occupations to women, including logistics, combat support, and air-tower control. Until just a few years ago, women still faced barriers to attending Command and Staff Colleges and National Defense University's War College, which are prerequisites for promotion. Those barriers have since been removed, allowing women to gain admittance to these institutes of higher learning alongside their male colleagues. Those women who do perform remarkable achievements in a military setting generally receive wide media attention. News of Taiwan's first female Army Ranger, for example, was effusive in its praise not just of Staff sergeant Hsieh Shu-chen (謝淑貞) after she successfully completed ranger training in 2013 — pointing out how she is considered just as tough as her male counterparts — but of the military itself, for having the dedication to equality and fairness for giving Hsieh the opportunity. A similar story followed the accomplishments of Second Lieutenant Hung Wan-ting (洪琬婷) of the ROC Military Academy who in 2007 became the first Taiwanese (indeed the first Asian) female to graduate from the venerated United States Military Academy, also known as West Point.

While these accomplishments are indeed laudable and the institutions of the military and government in Taiwan are to be congratulated for paying heed to issues of gender equality, they do somewhat smack of tokenism. Despite the fact that females have been serving in the ROC armed forces in one capacity or another for half a century, the number of women promoted to the level of flag officer is remarkably low. This is despite the fact that women generally score higher in entrance exams than their male counterparts, with evidence suggesting that they also outperform them as well. Despite this, the ROC armed forces remain the sort of organization where women lag behind in terms of postings and promotions compared to their male counterparts with equal seniority.

This phenomenon is especially prevalent in the case of female service members who are known by their superiors to be married. It is a standard consideration for promotion boards to consider whether giving a particular promotion to a female officer will create a conflict for that officer's time, and whether the demands that a family places on wives – especially in a culture as traditional as Taiwan's – will reduce that officer's reliability and efficiency. This glass ceiling is very much in evidence in the ROC military, with discrimination and lack of promotion parity all too often being the result.

Even after the opening up to women of the majority of military occupations which took place in the period of democratization, patriarchal attitudes died hard, and policies designed to make life easier for female recruits only served to place a barrier to acceptance by the male members of their units. For example, all members must stand duty watches on a 24-hour basis, and initially, women were exempted from standing watch, ostensibly for reasons of safety. Not only did men complain about being overworked, but the women likewise complained, arguing that they had not asked for special treatment. Eventually, administrators allowed women to serve duty shifts during the day, but they were still exempted from night shifts. Again, this served only to create a difference between service members of different genders and acted as a stumbling block to full acceptance and integration (Chen, 2009, p. 85).

When Ma Ying-jeou announced his intention of shifting to an All-Volunteer Force, it immediately became apparent to military planners that, if the easy task of staffing under conscription was going to give way to the much more difficult prospect of recruiting volunteers, the participation of women would be necessary to help make up recruitment shortfalls. Data for 2012 indicate that while a mere 68 percent of the targeted number of enlistees was met, all of the billets open to female recruits were filled. What's more, vying for those 799 billets were an astounding 5,300 female applicants. This, as much as any metric, represents how much Taiwan society leads its military in terms of female empowerment. By the end of 2013, females made up just 11 percent of enlisted personnel in the ROC armed forces. This may seem low, but it is still far ahead of the rates (between 3 and 4 percent) in Japan and South Korea, which share a similar Confucian-influenced

Figure 8.1. Opinion on Opening Military Jobs to Women.

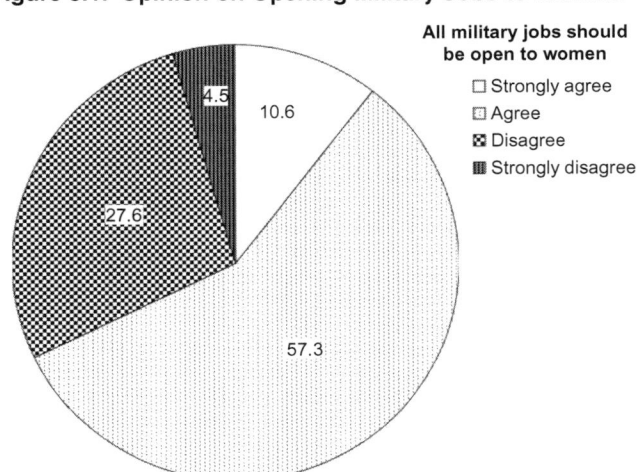

All military jobs should
be open to women

☐ Strongly agree
☐ Agree
☒ Disagree
▦ Strongly disagree

culture, and is not far behind the United States, at about 15 percent (South China Morning Post, 2013).

The way Taiwan citizens perceive this issue would seem to support this observation. The perception of women in uniform is not impacted significantly by self-identification. Indeed, the only significant predictor of the belief that all military jobs should be open to women is, perhaps not surprisingly, gender. The results of the research indicate that females tend to agree more that all military careers should be open to women, while overall, shown in Figure 8.1, 67.9 percent of respondents either agreed or strongly agreed with opening all jobs to females, against a mere 32.1 percent who disagreed or strongly disagreed.

CHAPTER 9

HOMOSEXUALS IN THE ROC MILITARY

There is no law or regulation permitting homosexuals to serve in the ROC military. On the other hand, this also means that there is no law or regulation expressly forbidding it, either. And while in practice, homosexual activity has been dealt with harshly by superiors and peers, on paper at least, homosexuals seem to be largely ignored in the ROC army, almost as much are they are genuinely accepted by Taiwan society. Thus this dimension can be assessed as being in the realm of the postmodern military. It has been said that Taiwan is not a "crusader culture," and therefore it is little surprise that there has been less interest in effecting big, loud, society-wide change on this issue, and more in just going along quietly. As evidence of this, survey results indicate that 58.5 percent of respondents expressed a preference for, essentially, a "don't ask, don't tell" policy. This in fact might best suit the needs of the ROC military, at least in the present generation, which appears to be caught between young people with a strong belief in the values of democracy and personal freedom, and a more conservative, traditionalist culture that views such values as a western import.

The issue of homosexuals serving in the ROC military has not received the frank discussion that it deserves, neither in the academic literature nor in wider society. For the AVF transition to be successful it will require the military's embrace of gender diversity. Taoism, Buddhism, and Confucianism have each had a great impact on the formation of Taiwan's value systems — both individually and as components of the largely syncretic belief system in Taiwan — and while they differ in many aspects, they share an emphasis on promoting collectivism over individualism. In this way, they tend to reinforce traditional military values. The Taoist concept of complementary forces (yin and yang) working in tandem to provide balance in a dynamic system is the basis of much Chinese philosophical thought and the eastern view of the universe. In many interpretations of this belief system, homosexuality is a divergence of this balanced duality, and therefore has no place in the military, or in society. Nevertheless, Taiwan is a remarkably tolerant society, especially in comparison to many Asian societies. In Brunei, Shariah laws have made homosexual acts illegal, and in parts of Indonesia (Aceh, in particular), such acts may be punished by lashing. Even among those cultures that share a Confucian-influenced worldview, being gay is dealt with harshly: in Singapore, gay sex acts are designated as "gross indecency" and risk a jail term of up to two years.

In contrast, homosexuals in Taiwan are, if not embraced, at least tolerated by society, with legislation protecting them from discrimination in the workplace. Moreover, the ROC Constitutional Court ruled in May of 2017 that, under the Constitution, same-sex couples have the right to marry. The Court set the Legislature a deadline of two years in which to include this right in the nation's marriage legislation. This represents a significant step forward, and while the move was not without its detractors, the majority of opposition came not from more traditionalist quarters, but from a small but vocal collection of Christian activists. Christians account for approximately 5 percent of the population, with Buddhism and Taoism — neither of which has any doctrinal opposition to homosexuality — making up the majority of the population. As a result, everyday life for homosexuals in Taiwan is more amenable than in other East Asian countries: there are a large number of bars, dance clubs, and bookstores that cater to a gay clientele, and public displays of affection rarely engender any negative reaction. Despite this societal tolerance, it is still difficult for many Taiwan homosexuals to find acceptance from family, which remains the most important societal unit in what is still a very traditional society. Gay men especially have strict demands from parents on their life choices — to find a traditional girl; to get married; to produce grandchildren — and it can be still very difficult to come out to parents (Jacobs, 2014).

With the 2016 election of Tsai Ing-wen as ROC president, gay rights advocates expressed high hopes that homosexual rights would be further expanded, as Tsai had, in the past, been vocal in her support of this cause. Even prior to the aforementioned court victory, same-sex couples in Taiwan could file as partners in their household registration, conferring certain rights to said couples. There remains progress yet to be made, however — in terms of social-housing rights, for example, and equal opportunities in the civil service. Moreover, law enforcement authorities tend, rightly or wrongly, to link the gay lifestyle to drug use and other undesirable activity, making it difficult to get the benefit of the doubt in interactions with the police and other authorities (Banning-Lover & Clarke, 2016).

Despite this openness, the military experience is unique in that young male conscripts are expected to train, eat, and work together, in close quarters. They are required to shower together, and bunk in the same barracks. This enforced closeness is an age-old military ritual that helps create a bond akin to brotherhood among the young men in the unit, which reinforces their collective identity as soldiers in a hypermasculine identification process. The presence of an openly-gay conscript in this equation threatens to upset the balance, and can open up that individual to teasing, unfair treatment, and greater difficulty being accepted as one of the group.

It is worth noting that this lack of acceptance of homosexuality within the ranks may be exacerbated in an All-Volunteer Force situation: Taiwan society, especially the younger generation, is remarkably tolerant of homosexuality, almost to the point of embracing it; and so long as the military's conscripts are sourced from this population, they will bring these views with them. A professional force, in contrast, would most likely be made up of a far greater percentage of those individuals who are attracted to the traditional military lifestyle, and eager to accept and internalize traditional military values. It is quite likely, therefore, that an AVF military, in a traditionally Confucian society, would be even less tolerant of homosexuality within its ranks.

There are no regulations overtly governing the issue of homosexuality or homosexual behavior in the ROC military, save for a brief 2002 proscription against homosexual applicants joining the ranks of the military police. It is worth noting that the policy was revised after being challenged by the media and by society in general (Palm Center, 2002). While this may prove to be a positive thing (there are no regulations banning it, for instance), the lack of regulatory direction can lead to problematic inconsistencies in the treatment of gay service members. Often this leads to homosexual behavior being adjudicated as cases of assault or molestation, and the dishonorable discharge of the individuals involved (Chen, 2009, p. 90).

9.1. RESEARCH FINDINGS

The vast majority of respondents (58.5 percent) expressed a preference for a "don't ask, don't tell" policy similar to what had been practiced in the US military until the turn of the century. An impressive 30.8 percent expressed the belief that homosexuals should be allowed to serve openly, while just 10.7 percent said they believed that homosexuals should be kicked out of the military. Overall, these results confirm what has already been observed and paint Taiwan as a nation that is remarkably tolerant of homosexuality — especially in comparison with its East Asian neighbors. By connecting with the media, popular culture, and postmodernism, gay/lesbian/queer movements on the island have succeeded in presenting their community as avant-garde, trendy, and the most progressive on the cultural front (Liou, 2006, p. 143). While Taiwan may be one of the most tolerant and gay-friendly societies in Asia, are such attitudes related to self-identification? (Figure 9.1).

A regression was run against the results using all previous predictors, and self-identification, as well as age, is indeed a factor, indicating that the younger one is, and the more one self-identifies as Taiwanese, the less likely one is to oppose the desire of homosexuals to serve openly in the military. Again, this result would seem to have face validity, as youth and self-identification as Taiwanese would both seem to carry with them an acceptance of liberal ideals and a rejection of the more conservative, even oppressive, concepts of "Asian values" which are often espoused by

Figure 9.1. Policy on Homosexuals in the Military.

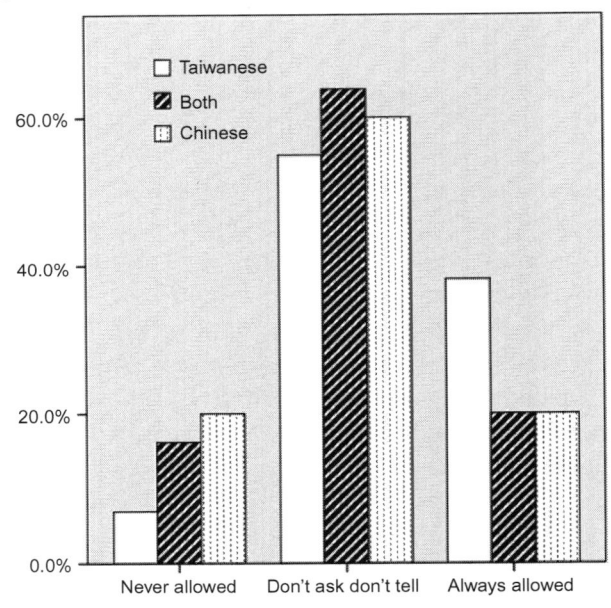

conservative regimes in the region as a rejection of what they see as western decadence, that is, human rights, excessive social liberties, tolerance of homosexuality, and often democracy.

CHAPTER 10

PUBLIC ATTITUDES AND MEDIA RELATIONS

10.1. PUBLIC ATTITUDES TOWARD THE ROC MILITARY

Survey results clearly demonstrate that there is ambivalence in the public's attitudes toward the ROC military, again arguing for placement in the late-modern era. To achieve the postmodern designation, in which public attitudes toward the military are marked by general indifference, would be impossible so long as so many people are directly affected by the military in the form of continued conscription: ensuring that every young man (not able to obtain a waiver) must don the uniform and potentially be put in harm's way, thereby affecting not only all these young men of conscription age, but their fathers, mothers, sisters, and every member of the family. Put succinctly, the people of Taiwan do not have the luxury of being indifferent to their military. Moreover, a large part of the ambivalence comes from the image of the military as a conservative, deep-blue institution in society, whereas society itself is split between those who sympathize with the pan-blue worldview of one day returning to the Chinese fold and the pan-green worldview of having a Taiwan for Taiwanese.

The public's attitude toward the ROC military can be viewed as having two distinct stages: that leading up to the lifting of martial law and the period of democratization in the 1980s, and that taking place after. In the former, the public's attitude was generally very supportive, due in no small part to propaganda and public relation efforts on the part of the military and government. In the post martial-law period, as holes began to form in the military's opacity, the prevailing public attitude shifted toward one of ambivalence.

In the KMT's early years in Taiwan, the military had a difficult task projecting a positive image for itself. The first KMT troops that arrived in Taiwan in 1945 following the Japanese surrender were generally young, uneducated, and battle-weary from years of fighting the Japanese. Upon their arrival on the island, they found a population of ostensibly Chinese compatriots but who were educated to speak Japanese: they dressed in the Japanese style, ate Japanese cuisine, and largely lived lives that were heavily influenced by Japanese customs. Initially, the Taiwanese welcomed Chinese rule, with but a few voices calling for independence or UN trusteeship (Roy, 2003, p. 110). Neither side developed an immediate affinity for the other, however, and to make matters worse, the troops soon set about looting Taiwan of its resources and infrastructure to be crated up and shipped to the mainland to aid in the ongoing war effort against the Communists. By the time the KMT retreated to Taiwan in 1949, the party and military had to find a way to improve their image and gain public support.

They did this by putting forward an image of the ROC military that was in direct opposition to how the public perceived the Communist regime in China — referring to the

Taipei regime as "Free China," for example, and keeping public attention fixed on the threat of invasion from across the strait. This PR effort was aided by events occurring in China, such as the disastrous Great Leap Forward and later the Cultural Revolution, in which all representations of traditional Chinese culture were targeted for death and destruction at the hands of uniformed gangs of fanatical Communist youths. In contrast, the ROC military seemed remarkably well disciplined and helpful.

To promote this image and gain public support, the military launched an agricultural assistance program whereby it dispatched soldiers to aid tenant farmers in bringing in their harvests. Remember, the ROC had lost China to a peasant uprising that was largely fueled by dissatisfaction with the division of wealth and opportunity, an inequitable class system, and all the other tropes that Communist ideology stands in opposition to. ROC leaders were not about to allow a similar uprising to occur in Taiwan by an equally disenfranchised class of tenant farmers. Thus, while this dynamic would soon be changed under the government's land reform and land-to-the-tiller programs, sending soldiers to aid tenant farmers in their labors was a stroke of genius. Not only did this program aid in shoring up the military's image, it contributed to the agricultural industry in Taiwan and earned praise from the farmers themselves – praise which quickly spread to the wider society.

Moreover, the threat from across the strait was ever-present, and the military was rightly positioned as the only practical defense against that threat. Public confidence in the army's ability to defend the country was boosted by victories such as the Battle of Kinmen in 1949, and later the Taiwan Strait Crisis which began in 1958 with the shelling of the outlying islands of Kinmen and Matsu. This shelling would continue, albeit in a less deadly form, until the late 1970s.

Another PR exercise performed by the military was an annual exercise that was conducted over half the island, and therefore very visible to the people, wherein troops would simulate a conflict between ROC soldiers and the PLA. This continued over a series of days, and while it impacted the perception of the population, troops were evaluated on their discipline and courtesy when interacting with civilians. Participants were under strict orders not to disturb the locals as they performed their duties, and in the rare cases when damage to individuals or property was incurred, the government would promptly make restitution. As a result, public perception of the military, as well as public confidence in their ability to defend against Chinese attack, increased.

In addition to these carefully managed interactions with the public, the military became adept at producing effective propaganda to boost its image. In addition to operating, in conjunction with the Ministry of Education, CTS, which disseminated patriotic programming, educational content related to anti-Communism, and other forms of political education in a far more entertaining way than Taiwan's only other two television stations, the MND produced a number of films that highlighted the courage of ROC soldiers in the war with Japan. These films were effective in inculcating a degree of trust in the military's ability to defend the nation, while promoting national unity and positive social values. Even through the 1970s, when the ROC was losing allies such as Japan and the United States, as well as losing its seat in the United Nations, such propaganda films helped to steel the population at a time when the ROC's position in the international community was faltering.

Of course, all these propaganda and public relation efforts were successful because the military operated in a way that was not transparent, thus allowing military leaders to effectively manage potentially scandalous events, such as training deaths and corruption, keeping them away from the public eye. This began to change in the 1980s during Taiwan's democratization, as the media was unleashed from government control and the military's influence in the KMT party was diminished.

With the lifting of martial law in 1987 came an increase in the number of media outlets, and the airing of opposing viewpoints, making it harder for the military to manage its image than it had been in the past. In addition to voices now openly promoting Taiwan independence, there were people who blamed the KMT government for losing the UN seat to China, and for mishandling the diplomatic tug-of-war for international recognition, and the military − still seen by many as the party army − bore the brunt of this criticism at least as much as the KMT itself did. Moreover, ethnic divisions between the Benshengren and the Waishengren came to the fore, now that the strong hand of the Chiang regime no longer suppressed their expression. Cleavages that began to form as early as 1947 with the 228 incident, but which found no expression, began to define Taiwan's struggle for identity in the vacuum created by the KMT's releasing grip.

These ethnic cleavages have a direct impact on the public perception of the military because of the military's historical close ties with the KMT party, and as such, it is seen as a blue institution. Indeed, even as the KMT itself underwent a degree of Taiwanization in the 1980s and 1990s, the military was left espousing the "old guard" view on the independence vs unification question, and thus painted itself into a corner as regards its political stance. This led to distrust by society and a loss of public support. Making matters even more difficult, this was taking place at a time when advancements in communications technologies were making it increasingly more difficult for military leadership to keep potentially embarrassing incidents under wraps. Whereas in the past, a training accident or a sex scandal could be kept out of the papers by a compliant media, in the modern era informants could email or text-message details and photographs directly to a media now focused on scare quotes and sensationalistic headlines.

When the actual frequency of conscript deaths became known to the public, there was a loss of confidence not only in the military's ability to defend the nation, but also in its ability to investigate such incidents fairly and impartially. The Association of Promotion of Human Rights in the Military (APHRM) was founded in 1995 as a watchdog group with the aim of publicizing these incidents and pressuring the military to clean up its act. Huang Hua-hsi, a legislative assistant, was quoted in an Asia Times Online report as saying that Taiwanese people generally had little confidence in the combat capabilities of their own military. He added that while many take the threat of attack from China "rather fatalistically," this should not be interpreted to mean that they want to give up on an appropriate defense (Kastner, 2011).

Reasoning that what has worked in the past might just work again, the military began addressing its PR problem in part by shifting its mission focus from one of defense to one that included a great deal more military operations other than war (MOOTW), especially HA/DR operations. Like the agricultural assistance program, this puts military members in public view, visibly contributing to relief and assistance efforts in times of national disaster. In the 9/21 earthquake that rocked Taiwan in 1999, causing 2,416 deaths and wounding 11,443 people, soldiers were quickly dispatched to aid in SAR efforts. In the many natural disasters that have struck Taiwan since, the military has consistently deployed SAR and other personnel to aid the government in its emergency management efforts, resulting in an improvement of its image among the local population. Moreover, despite

Taiwan's increasing economic reliance on China, many remained unconvinced of that country's "peaceful rise" and worried that Beijing may yet make good on its desire to annex the island, by force if necessary. Increasingly belligerent moves against other claimants to islands in the South China Sea, for example, as well as Beijing's passage of the Anti-Secession Law in 2005, are constant reminders to the people of Taiwan that a large, well-funded, and well-equipped military is sitting on their doorstep waiting for an excuse to invade. The only thing stopping that from happening, notwithstanding ROC government efforts to placate China economically, is the ROC military. This knowledge goes a long way toward mitigating some of the loss of public support experienced in the era of democratization (Chen, 2009, p. 76).

In terms of whether citizens have faith in the military's ability to defend Taiwan from attack, overall more than half of the respondents lack such faith (**Figure** 10.1). Looking closer, it would seem that the younger the respondent, the

Figure 10.1. Faith in the Military's Ability to Defend Taiwan.

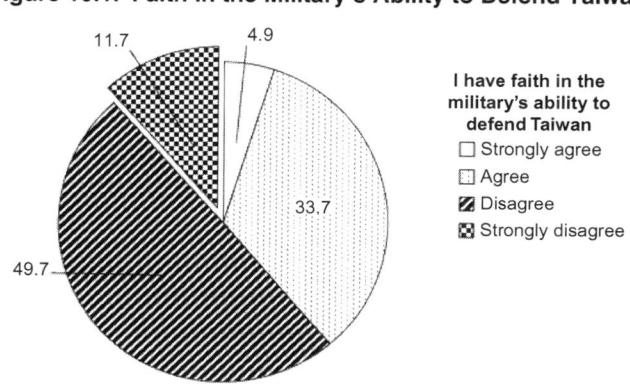

less faith he has in the military. Moreover, results also show that the more one has Chinese heredity and identity (in terms of both Mainlander parental background and self-identification as Chinese), the less faith one has in the military, as seen in **Table 10.1**. Of course, this can be read it the reverse way as well: the older one is and the more one has a Taiwanese family background and identity, the more faith one has in the military to defend Taiwan from attack. Clearly, faith in the military's ability to defend Taiwan is impacted significantly by self-identification. A related factor in this result could be that, as previously discussed, persons self-identifying as Taiwanese are more likely to worry about the China threat than their counterparts who identify as Chinese, and hence put a greater premium on this task of the military's.

In the wake of several high-profile incidents of training accidents, especially in which personnel lose their lives, there is an overwhelming lack of faith in the military's handling of such cases, with 63.8 percent saying they disagree or strongly disagree with the statement that the military is fair and impartial when investigating cases in which young conscripts die during training (**Figure 10.2**). Clearly, there is ambivalence in attitudes toward the military. In seeking policy prescriptions, especially for efforts to render the ROC military more responsive to the people of Taiwan and more trustworthy in their eyes, it is important to know the degree to which the people of Taiwan actually believe that the military should, in fact, be such an institution. As Moskos has amply demonstrated, militaries can be of society or separate from the society they serve: they can be occupational or institutional. Before crafting a new societal role for the military, it is important to know where that society feels the military belongs.

Table 10.1. Faith in the Military to Defend Taiwan, by Ethnicity.

Model		Unstandardized Coefficients		Standardized Coefficients	t	Sig.
		B	Std. Error	Beta		
1	(Constant)	−18.031	5.970		−3.020	0.003
	Gender	−0.050	0.067	−0.034	−0.747	0.456
	Year of birth	0.010	0.003	0.172	3.359	0.001
	Parents' ethnic background[b]	0.061	0.029	0.100	2.091	0.037
	Educational level[c]	0.032	0.021	0.071	1.502	0.134
	Ethnic self-identification[d]	0.172	0.069	0.125	2.477	0.014

Notes: [a]Dependent Variable: I have faith in the military's ability to defend Taiwan from attack.

[b]Neither parent from mainland = −2; one parent from mainland = 0; both parents from mainland = 2.

[c]Illiterate up to post grad.

[d]Taiwanese = 1; both = 2; Chinese = 3.

Figure 10.2. Fairness and Impartiality of the Military.

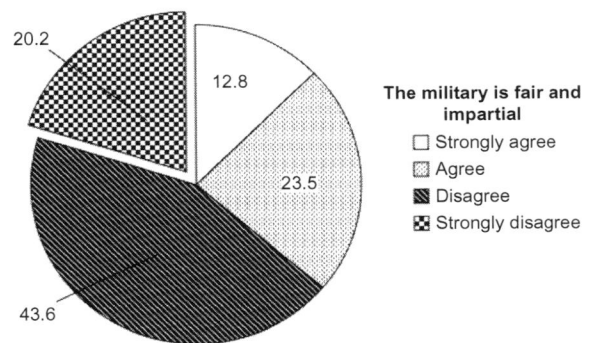

Survey results show that those who self-identify more as Chinese demonstrate significantly increased odds of holding the belief that it is not necessary for the military to reflect society's values, whereas those who identify as Taiwanese tend to think that the military should reflect society's values. This result offers insight into how each group views the military: with those self-identifying as Chinese seeing the role of the military to serve society, but not be of it. Considering that Taiwanese society today is one marked by a high degree of localization and increasingly one marked by identification as Taiwanese, this result fits in well with what is already known of the military's former (and vestigial) role as gatekeeper of KMT (read: Chinese) culture. Thus, as self-identifying Chinese see their numbers and influence in society dwindling year by year, it is reasonable to understand why they would not want the military to reflect the new values of the emerging Taiwanese society. Likewise, self-identifying Taiwanese who are benefiting from their worldview gaining prominence in an increasingly localizing (de-Sinicizing) culture would naturally seem to want a military that reflects their emergent society rather than the one that is still too identified with being the KMT army.

10.2. MEDIA RELATIONS WITH THE ROC MILITARY

Strictly speaking, the military courts the media in Taiwan today, ranking it in the postmodern era. Looking closer, however, there appears to be an antagonistic relationship between much of Taiwan's media and the military. Moreover, the power relationship has inverted: whereas the military once wielded so much power in society that it essentially controlled the media accounts of military (and indeed, non-military) matters, today the media has much more power to influence public perception of military issues. Indeed, many in the media seem to gleefully report on errors and scandals in the military ranks – beyond the true tragedies, such as training deaths and the like. There are many reasons for this, not least of which is the freedom enjoyed by the media today, as well as the competition for an audience, meaning that scandal and death sell more papers – following the age-old western newspaper adage: "if it bleeds, it leads." The military makes an easy target for this sort of sensationalistic media, not only because the nature of the military's operations are inherently dangerous and hence more likely to experience accidents and deaths, but also because of the secrecy and opacity with which the military inevitably tries to handle such occurrences, thus giving the reporters who break the story the frisson of having exposed a big secret.

During the period of martial law in Taiwan, both the military and the media were controlled by the KMT, through the Enforcement Rules for the Publications Act of 1952. Freedom of the press did not exist as such, and the government permitted only a few media outlets. The three TV stations which operated in Taiwan — CTS, China Television Company (CTV), and Taiwan Television Enterprise (TTV) — were all state-run, and thus the relationship with the military was very much one of tight incorporation. This is especially true in the case of the aforementioned CTS, which was essentially under the direct control of the military's General Political Warfare Department, which used the channel to disseminate patriotic programming, educational content related to anti-Communism, and other forms of political education.

Launched in 1971, CTS was a cooperative enterprise between the Ministries of Education and of National Defense, and was the third of the three aforementioned TV stations, both of which were also dedicated to pro-government programming, though they were widely regarded as having a lack of talent (TTV) and being "like a boring classroom" (the MOE-run CTS). Thus the CTS benefited from this vacuum in quality programming, as well as from the military's experience in producing political programming and training. Its initial leadership was in fact made up of retired officers from the General Political Warfare Department (Bullard, 1997, p. 112). The CTS operated very much as an arm of the military's and the government's political socialization efforts, thus contributing to better social control by the state and, indirectly, the maintenance of military stability and loyalty to the party (Chen, 2009, p. 79).

Such unabashed government control over media is unbecoming of a properly functioning democracy, and so by the advent of Taiwan's democratization stage, this was beginning to change, albeit this had less to do with the operation of media outlets and more to do with changes taking place in the military and the party. For example, one of the mechanisms through which the party and military were so tightly integrated was that almost a third of seats in the KMT Central Standing Committee were held by military officers.

These seats were removed by the 14th National Congress in 1993, concomitant with a Taiwanization of the party's ruling bodies, reflected in 112 of that committee's 210 members being native Taiwanese that year (Chang & Tien, 1996, p. 117). While the military was no longer able to exert as much influence on the direction of the party, it remained the nominal head of CTS and held the majority of shares in the channel. The real change in media relations would come in 1987, with the lifting of martial law.

With the end of martial law and direct government control over the media, a host of news and information outlets appeared, many of which were operated by the Tangwai opposition, which devoted significant coverage to the anti-democratic nature of the KMT. These opposition-run magazines and radio stations painted the ROC military as the KMT party's army, complicit in keeping the one-party state in power through the years of repression. Meanwhile, as the KMT itself underwent a degree of localization among its membership and leadership, the military, which remained largely run by Mainlanders, took upon itself the task of pushing back against the trend toward Taiwan independence. Advocating national unity, it was the military, more than the KMT itself, that was on the front lines of the ideological battle between independence and unification. In many ways, this established the military as the primary target for independence-minded opposition-run media outlets.

The newly-freed media was itself undergoing changes at this time. Not only were media organizations, which for decades only knew how to parrot government propaganda, suddenly given free rein to report as they pleased, but a host of new outlets formed, many of which had little journalistic experience to lean on, or whose experience was restricted to underground operations during the martial law era. In such a fiercely competitive market, the preferred method to gain market share has been to put a premium on sensationalistic or violent stories. Moreover, there remains even today very little in the way of investigative journalism practiced in Taiwan.

Not surprisingly, an ideological polarization coalesced in the wake of this untrammeled growth, with the increasingly vast media landscape in Taiwan falling into one of two camps: pro-blue or pro-green. Even though the government passed a law in 2003 requiring the government and political parties to divest themselves of media assets, and blocking government and party officials from sitting on the boards of media companies (the Satellite Broadcasting Act), in reality most media outlets are owned or controlled by wealthy private families or corporations that are unabashedly sympathetic to one side or another. Thus the coverage available through any single media outlet in Taiwan is unlikely to be fair and balanced.

In this media environment, the military could do little more than enter into a relationship of manipulation, successful at least with ideologically friendly media, since the end of martial law. This relationship shifted to one of the military courting the media by the late 1990s and early 2000s, as the media's autonomy grew and the competition for audiences became fierce. Today's media has little interest in military training or morale, and indeed, the "if it bleeds, it leads" mentality has resulted in a prevailing military coverage that focuses on scandals and accidental deaths. Thanks to advancements made in communications technology, the operation of the military is not as opaque as it once was, and it becomes harder for the Defense Ministry to put a cap on potentially embarrassing stories, the way it once did. Nevertheless, the slow pace of change within military leadership contributes to this "cover-up" mentality being the first avenue of action when the media seizes on a potentially embarrassing event. In many cases, the cover-up itself then becomes a scandal in a cycle that only serves to exacerbate the military's image problem.

Today, military efforts to court positive coverage from the media include hosting tours of bases and providing reporters with front-row seats for military exercises such as the annual Han Kuang Exercise. This transformed relationship indeed follows the postmodern military model, though how much of this is due to an evolution of thinking on the part of the military, and how much is due to the sea changes that have occurred in the media landscape, is a question worthy of discussion.

Given this relationship, it is important to determine the degree to which the general population believes this harsh coverage is justified, or whether people think that the military does not deserve to be treated so shabbily by the media. Survey results show that the more strongly one identifies as Taiwanese, the less likely he is to view the media as being unfair to the military in its coverage (**Figure 10.3**).

Thus, it is clear that perception of the media's coverage of the military is impacted significantly by self-identification: Those who self-identify as Taiwanese believe that the media harshness is warranted in covering the military. This is consistent with the observation that the military is widely seen as being antithetical to the push for independence, or at least localization. Moreover, given the control that the military exerted over the media in years past, it is possible that the population sees the pendulum as having swung the other way, with a free (albeit immature) media environment in the era of Taiwan democratization wielding more control over the public and playing a larger part in society than the once all-powerful ROC military. Moreover, it is exactly the kind of coverage provided by today's media that can conceivably apply pressure on the military to become more

Figure 10.3. Opinion on Media Coverage of the Military.

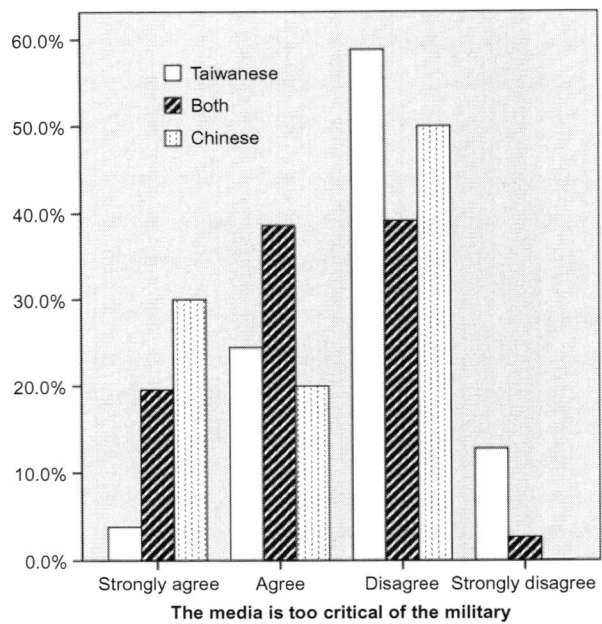

accountable in the eyes of the population: one which, as we have seen, may have respect for the military's defensive role, but not for how top brass manages the institution; and which would like to see a military that better reflects their values. How better to achieve that than through public pressure, in which the media plays an indispensable role.

CHAPTER 11

SUMMARY OF FINDINGS

This study is aimed at assessing the ROC military using the PMMM according to the perceptions of the citizens of Taiwan. Previous chapters have examined how the results of this research elucidate citizen's perceptions of the ROC military according to the dimensions of the PMMM, and the following table (Table 11.1) is a summary of those results in the form of descriptive statistics.

What patterns can be detected in Taiwan's military as regards the PMMM? For one thing, it paradoxically spans three distinct stages: the modern, late modern, and postmodern. This is not to imply that other nations' militaries fit squarely into one single categorization. Quite the opposite. Nevertheless, they all seem to follow a similar progression toward postmodernism, different only by degree.

Taiwan's is a modern military in terms of perceived threat, force structure, major mission definition, and civilian employees. It can be regarded as more of a late-modern model in the dimensions of dominant military professional, public attitude,

Table 11.1. Descriptive Statistics.

	N	Minimum	Maximum	Mean	Std. Deviation	Skewness	
	Statistic	Statistic	Statistic	Statistic	Statistic	Statistic	Std. Err
Gender[a]	501	1	2	1.43	0.495	0.287	0.109
Year of birth	501	1,915	1,995	1,971.57	12.374	−0.625	0.109
Ethnic self-identification[b]	500	1	3	1.43	0.534	0.686	0.109
Position unification/independence[c]	440	1.00	5.00	3.3591	0.86077	−0.290	0.116
Political preference[d]	361	0	1	0.46	0.499	0.162	0.128
Threat perception[e]	484	0.00	1.00	0.8140	0.38947	−1.619	0.111
Main military mission[f]	479	1	5	1.66	0.845	1.354	0.112
Faith in military to defend Taiwan	489	1	4	2.68	0.741	−0.138	0.110

Media too critical of the military	488	1	4	2.58	0.791	−0.370	0.111
Military jobs should be open to women	492	1	4	2.26	0.703	0.364	0.110
Openness to homosexuals[g]	487	1	3	2.20	0.612	−0.144	0.111
Policy on conscription[h]	476	0	1	0.76	0.430	−1.198	0.112
Policy on conscientious objection[i]	439	1	4	2.11	0.915	1.039	0.117
Valid N (listwise)	257						

[a]*Notes:* 1 = male; 2 = female.

[b]Taiwanese (1); both (2); or Chinese (3).

[c]Unification =1 to independence = 5.

[d]Blue = 1; green = 0.

[e]Threat is China = 1; Threat is a country other than Taiwan = 0.

[f]Defend against attack from China = 1; Defend against attack from another country = 2; Search and Rescue = 3; Humanitarian relief = 4; Assist allies =5.

[g]Not open =1; "don't ask, don't tell" =2; always allowed = 3.

[h]End conscription = 0; Keep conscription = 1.

[i]CO should never be allowed = 1 to CO should be allowed for any reason = 4.

and women's role. Lastly, it achieves a postmodern designation as regards the role of spouses, homosexuals, conscientious objection, and media relations. In all, this paints a picture of a fractured military culture: one between two worlds. This should not be surprising: to many in Taiwan, Taiwan itself is a fractured culture, seeking to define its identity, and find its place in the world, and in history.

A closer look at these results, however, reveals some intriguing patterns. In the dimensions in which Taiwan rates as a modern military, we can see this is driven by external factors. The geopolitical scenario in which the nation finds itself, that is, under threat of invasion by a numerically and technologically superior foe, is very much a pre-Cold War scenario for most of the rest of the world. Therefore, dimensions such as perceived threat, force structure, and major mission definition all reflect that reality, and appropriately so. It should be noted that were it not for Taiwan's diplomatic isolation and the lack of active-duty combat deployments, the dimension of dominant military professional would, in all likelihood, be rated as modern as well, with higher ranks being filled by combat leaders.

It exhibits a late-modern model in the dimensions of public attitude and women's role, and a PMMM when it comes to the role of spouses, homosexuals, conscientious objection, and media relations — all factors that are related primarily to how the military interacts with the society it protects. Thus, we have a bifurcated profile for the ROC military, yet not an inappropriate one. The ROC military must, as it does, focus on a modern-era threat perception, just as it must, as it does, focus on a postmodern-era approach to women and homosexuals in the military (see Table 11.2).

Table 11.2 is a summary of the assessment of the ROC military using the dimensions of the PMMM, which illustrates how the aforementioned bifurcation is expressed. Rows

Table 11.2. Summary: Taiwan and the Postmodern Military Model.

PMMM Dimension	Characteristic	Era	Driver
Perceived threat	Enemy invasion	Modern	Geopolitics
Major mission definition	Defense of homeland	Modern	Geopolitics
Civilian employees	Minor component	Modern	Geopolitics
Force structure	Conscription	Modern	Geopolitics
Public attitude	Ambivalent	Late modern	Society
Women's role	Partial integration	Late modern	Society
Dominant military professional	Manager/ Technician	Late modern	Geopolitics
Media relations	Courted	Postmodern	Society
Spouses	Removed	Postmodern	Society
Homosexuals in the military	Ignored	Postmodern	Society
Conscientious objection	Alternative service	Postmodern	Society

tinted dark represent dimensions that fit a modern military; rows tinted lightly represent a postmodern representation; and those with a median tint represent late-modern dimensions. What immediately becomes clear is that the dimensions that are primarily driven by geopolitics (to wit, the China threat) are assessed as being consistent with that of a modern military, whereas those which are driven primarily by society (i.e., family roles and tolerance of homosexuals) are consistent with a postmodern society. This is a reflection of the competing influences driving the evolution of military—society relations in Taiwan: on the one hand, the threat is one that requires a modern-era military to confront it, and on the other is a rapidly changing society that demands a postmodern approach from its institutions. How can this challenge be answered? Not by blindly adopting the solutions employed in other countries, especially the West. These solutions cannot accommodate the unique needs, as illustrated here, of the ROC military, and will inevitably be found wanting.

11.1. JAPAN, CHINA, AND THE KOREAS

Very little formal research has been conducted with respect to using Moskos's PMMM to analyze the militaries in East Asia. Each of the nations in this region, namely Japan, China, and North and South Korea, has a military that, for one reason or another, does not lend itself to easy categorization, especially using a model derived for use primarily based on the Western post-WWII experience.

Japanese society's relationship with its military is a complex one, given the history of imperial aggression in the region and the pacifist constitution imposed by the United States that severely restricts the operation of the military. Article 9 of the Japanese Constitution, for example, enunciates a complete renunciation of war and bars the deployment of assets anywhere outside the country. Indeed, even the terms "Army," "Navy," and "Air Force." Are not used, with these service branches instead being referred to as the "Japan Ground Self-Defense Force," the "Japan Maritime Self-Defense Force," and the "Japan Air Self-Defense Force." Clearly, self-defense is the operative concept. The reason for this is so that Japan could never again engage in the colonial and war-making behavior it exhibited in the late 19th and early 20th centuries. As a consequence of this history, Japanese society continues to have a strong anti-military posture even today, and nationalism and patriotism are not esteemed values (Arrington, 2002; Kurashina, 2003).

Despite the aforementioned Article 9, Japanese military units began taking part in peacekeeping operations in the 1990s, mostly in logistical and support roles, and mostly in support of the nation's primary ally, the United States. This and an increased focus on HA/DR helped to ameliorate the military's image among the Japanese populace, and renders it unsuitable for description using the PMMM. This is not to say that the Japanese military has not undergone transformation: The Japanese military as it existed during the two decades following 1995 could best be described as a "proscribed postmodern military," or more accurately as a "cosmopolitan army" (Hunter-Chester, 2016). Moreover, according to Japanese scholars, it is unlikely that the nation's military will be allowed the luxury of transforming into a full-fledged postmodern military of the type described by Moskos, due largely to the continuing threat that exists as a result of the situation on the Korean Peninsula. This threat is analogous to the China threat facing Taiwan and preventing the ROC military from making the leap into the postmodern era (Funabashi, 2002).

As with Japan, there has been little academic effort to apply the PMMM to the military in South Korea, save for an enlightening 2009 doctoral dissertation by researcher Kijoo Kim, whose findings indicate that the South Korean experience does not conform to the PMMM. While Kim acknowledges that the PMMM is a useful analytical tool, serving as a comprehensive framework with which to examine military organizations and the relationship between the South Korean military and society, he identified rather three explanatory variables to explain civil—military relations and military type in South Korea. These variables are threat perception, political change, and social values.

Nevertheless, the researcher concludes that South Korea's military can be seen as moving toward a postmodern military. There are a number of reasons for this, such as the increasing dominance of soldier—scholars, for example. In other dimensions, it ranks as a late-modern military, such as the trend toward civilianization of the military and the public's attitude having shifted from supportive to ambivalent. The South Korean military's assessment according to the PMMM is not unlike that of Taiwan, due largely to the continuing threat from North Korea, which is akin to the cross-strait situation. Military-dependent variables (force structure, major mission definition, and dominant military professional) in both cases are largely influenced primarily by this threat and therefore conform to what Moskos identified as a modern military, whereas the sociological dependent variables (public attitude toward military, media—military relations, civilian employees, and the role of military wives in the military community, and the integration or acceptance of women, conscientious objectors, and homosexuals in the military) score more toward the postmodern military, as they are influenced by the advancements made in society and concerned with the military's credibility and legitimacy in society (Kim, 2009).

The final two nations in the East Asian region, China and North Korea, both remain communist states and hence the state of civil—military does not lend itself to assessment using the PMMM, although China's vast wealth and enormous military spending has allowed the PLA to modernize significantly over the past two decades, exhibiting some developments — in officer education, for example — that on the surface appear to hint at a move in the postmodern direction (Bickford, 2007).

Arguably, the issue on which this topic is perhaps most impactful in Taiwan – the push for an AVF transition – straddles the line between the two competing influences of military-dependent variables and sociological dependent variables. The issue of conscription fits into the category of force structure; and as a staffing and manpower issue, this dimension is the one that is best suited for an analysis of the issue within the rubric of the PMMM. The decision of whether or not to employ conscription as a means of maintaining a large standing force capable of defending against the threat of attack is clearly a decision driven by the geopolitical nature of that threat. And yet as a program that would affect nearly every household (and does affect every male) in the nation, it is also greatly influenced by society and the direction in which society is evolving. Therefore, on the one hand, while conscription is still needed for staffing purposes and basic defense, there is a temptation to eliminate it in order to achieve a truly postmodern society. The following chapter will examine the soundness of that idea in the context of Taiwan.

CHAPTER 12

POLICY RECOMMENDATIONS

12.1. THE MORALE PROBLEM

Despite vows by newly-elected President Tsai Ing-wen to address the problem of low morale among the armed forces, very little has been accomplished. The 2017 National Defense Report released on December 26, 2017 reiterates the military's commitment to the AVF transition, the indigenous development of military aircraft and warships, and the desire to implement a defense posture based on "strong defense and layered deterrence," which involves using "innovative and asymmetrical warfare" to confront the enemy with multiple dilemmas to achieve deterrence. Unfortunately, the document does little more than pay lip service to the issue of morale.

This low morale is expressed in a number of ways, and has a multitude of causes. The size of the armed forces has shrunk significantly, for example, from 400,000 in 1996 to well under 200,000 today, and while the number of reservists on paper is significant, very little is asked of them. In addition to being underequipped, they are rarely if ever called up for training, and most are not even assigned to actual units (Wu, 2017).

Moreover, under Tsai, there has been little reversal of the trend for retired or active ROC military personnel implicated in espionage for China. A recent case highlighted by an editorial in *The Taipei Times* involved a retired colonel surnamed Lan from Pingtung County charged with offenses against state security. Despite a raft of international precedents for governments to restrict the travel of certain segments of the population to sensitive nations (Moscow bans many Russian citizens from traveling overseas, for example, and Americans still face travel restrictions on such nations as Cuba), the Tsai administration has not introduced similar legislation that would help curb such espionage. While the loss of sensitive information to the enemy is potentially disastrous, the deleterious effect on troop morale is no less debilitating to the armed forces.

Finally, the way conscription has been handled signals to those called up that even their superiors view it as a bureaucratic inconvenience rather than an essential component of the nation's defense. Not only has mandatory service been reduced to four months (from a high of two years) — far too short a time to inculcate a spirit of esprit de corps, much less transfer necessary soldiering skills — the avenues of "alternative service" have expanded to allow men of serving age to meet their commitments as competitive video gamers and convenience-store employees. The message is clear: serving as a uniformed member of the armed forces is less well regarded than wearing the uniform of a 7-Eleven clerk.

12.2. THE ALL-VOLUNTEER FORCE TRANSITION

How can policymakers make use of the information presented here? For a start, it is worth reexamining the impulse to make the AVF shift. In large part, it stems from a desire to use what has worked in other countries, particularly America, from which the ROC derives many institutional and policy models. In the current situation, there has been an effort to apply the American example of the AVF transition to the ROC military. A closer look at the experience of the United States military and the conditions therein immediately prior to and during the transition reveals several differences that, at best, make the application of the American model problematic and, at worst, conspire to sabotage the entire effort. The following is a look at some of those factors as enunciated by a study conducted by the Rand Corp. and an analysis of how each is applicable to conditions in Taiwan.

A Political Imperative: Campaigning for President in 1968, Richard Nixon made the transition to AVF a platform of his election campaign – an issue that saw significant opposition within the military. In many ways, this parallels the experience in Taiwan, where Ma Ying-jeou, campaigning for president 40 years later, made a similar campaign promise in his own bid for president – the idea likewise facing opposition from the ROC military. Both men won office, but this is where the similarity ends. In Taiwan, an attempt was immediately made to implement the plan. Initial attempts failed due largely to a lack of adequate funding from the government, and the deadline for implementation was delayed first to 2014, and then again to 2016. The reasons for the failure of the transition thus far shall be examined in more detail, but they stem from two main causes: the failure to draw up and follow a detailed plan for the transition, and the failure of the government to provide the promised support, especially in the form of adequate funding.

In contrast, in the United States, Nixon did not immediately engage in implementing the transition, and instead first commissioned a report to study its feasibility and methods of implementation. This became known as the Gates Commission Report. This report provided a detailed blue-print on how to implement the transition, and it should be noted that it was steeped in the occupation model on the institutional/occupational spectrum. It is worth remembering that conscription is not an American norm or tradition, historically speaking. Indeed, in its approximately 240 years of history, the United States employed conscription for a mere 35 years – most of which was in the decades immediately prior to the AVF transition.

Demographics: By the time of the Nixon administration, the population of draft-age young men in the United States was far larger than the manpower requirements of the military at that time. This served as an incentive to shifting the focus to a leaner, more professional volunteer military. In contrast, demographics are not in Taiwan's favor. According to the information website Index Mundi (providing numbers for year 2017), the birth rate is 8.3 births/1,000 population, with a total fertility rate of 1.13. This is a very low fertility scenario with grave implications for Taiwan's population growth, especially given the culture's traditional aversion to immigration intake (with a net migration rate of 0.9 migrants/1,000 population). With a median age of 40.7 and a population growth rate of just 0.17 percent, this paints the picture of a graying population with all the associated problems that that entails.

As a result, the exact opposite demographic conditions are at play in Taiwan than were at the time of the US transition, with too few eligible young men to meet the needs of military staffing. Likewise, the nation's universities are also finding that demographics are responsible for a drop in matriculation rates, and hence tuition revenues. As a result, they are turning to accepting large numbers of exchange students from China to fill the gap — clearly an option that is not available to the military.

Cost: The United States had the budget to hire enough volunteers, and to offer salaries and benefits that were comparable to what applicants could make working in the civilian sector. In contrast, Taiwan's effort to transition to a professional military is suffering from budget shortfalls. Another of the campaign promises made by Ma Ying-jeou was to commit to defense spending of no less than 3 percent of GDP. According to the CIA World Factbook, however, ROC military expenditures were 2.2 percent of GDP in 2012, and the government further reduced the budget (from US$ 10.6 billion to US$ 10.5 billion) in 2013. At the time of writing, the country's most recent budget (2017) showed that defense spending still hovered around 2 percent of GDP, or US$ 10.5 billion. Like Ma before her, Tsai promised to boost defense spending to 3 percent of GDP, and like Ma before her, she has so far failed to deliver. From a fiscal standpoint, the AVF initiative is in dire straits.

Moral Considerations: Both sides of the political aisle called for an end to the draft in America, with those on the left decrying the overrepresentation of Blacks and other underprivileged members of American society in the ranks of the conscript US army, while libertarians and the right opposed the very notion of the state forcing young men to do its fighting without their consent.

Taiwan has no clear-cut analogy to these positions. While there is the Chinese tradition of conscription dating back to the Warring States period, conscription of Taiwan's young men into the ROC army has been in place since 1949. The moral component is a difficult one to convey, and it is imperative that different viewpoints seeing the issue very differently be measured before making any radical shifts in policy. From the perspective of the ROC elite – the Mainlanders who came to Taiwan in 1949 with the KMT party, the government, the ROC military, and the various institutions and individuals who feared death at the hands of Mao's Communists – is there a moral conundrum at all? After all, they view the Taiwanese people as fellow Chinese, and as such, it is perfectly natural to expect that they should serve in the army of the ROC. On the other hand, there are many in Taiwan who do not consider themselves Chinese at all, preferring to self-identify as Taiwanese: their view of conscription in the army of the ROC (or worse, of the KMT, should the military not be able to shed that image) is different. As evidenced by this research, very few respondents indicated an inclination toward promoting a military career to their sons and daughters.

Opposition to the Vietnam War: While popular opposition to the war in Vietnam was undoubtedly one of the motivating factors behind the US administration's desire to end conscription, this too has no direct parallel in Taiwan. While arguably no active state of war exists between Taiwan and China, the latter constitutes a serious threat to the security of the island, and has made its intention of annexing the island, by force if necessary, very clear. Naturally, this differs greatly from the Vietnam situation America found itself in, with Taiwan here being the party open to a potential invasion, and therefore in need of defending. Thus many find it odd that this moment should be chosen for an effort to end conscription on the island. However, given the nature of Taiwan politics and the complex cross-strait relationship, there is little wonder that this project should be proposed by the administration of Ma Ying-jeou, who had been trying since being elected ROC president to smooth relations with Beijing and oversee a rapprochement between the two countries. Ma's policies showed a trend toward an avoidance of riling Beijing, and strong efforts to put the Taiwan/China relationship above all others. Thus, it is little wonder that his administration would take steps to downgrade the overt lethality and capacity of the ROC military, as it stands in the way of other cross-strait policies driven by "soft-power." Moreover, the KMT party itself has a recent history of neglect of the military, as evidenced by its actions of using its control of the Legislative Yuan to boycott weapons purchases no fewer than 51 times during the entire eight-year tenure of President Chen Shui-bian – eight years during which the PLA gained a sizeable advantage over the ROC military.

The US Army had a Desire for Change: This point is related to the previous one, with the war in Vietnam being responsible for a large number of discipline problems among draftees who, quite understandably, did not want to be there. It was thought by army generals that a more capable army made up of professional soldiers would not suffer from these problems, and so the time had come for a change. While it is likewise time for a change in Taiwan as well, the radically differing challenges and conditions between the two countries and eras mean that the changes adopted must also be different. How then shall policymakers and social leaders chart an appropriate course for the future development of the ROC military? One thing is certain: it must take local realities and conditions into account.

12.3. A NEW MILITARY ETHIC

The paragraphs that follow propose some suggestions for future areas of military policy that are not solid policy recommendations per se so much as they are ideas for programs and projects that would help to usher in a new organizational culture within the ROC military in ways that will help alleviate some of the problems (i.e., media relations, public perception) that, as identified in this volume, beset today's military. As discussed earlier, it is inadvisable to implement policy without first conducting research into how best to do so; how similar policies have been implemented in other militaries; and how best to adapt the experience of others to suit the unique cultural conditions in Taiwan. Thus, while these represent potential policy goals, each also represents the potential for further research.

Focus on the Land: The ethic and character of the ROC military is very much focused on the ideals expounded by Dr. Sun Yat-sen and the Three Principles of the People. While these are laudable ethical underpinnings for an organization with its roots in China, they are, as previously mentioned, anachronistic in today's Taiwan, and do not represent the values of modern young people. While there is very little agreement among the nation's ethnic groups and political philosophies, there is one thing that unites Taiwan people of all stripes, be they Hoklo or Hakka, Mainlander or Taiwanese, and indigenous person or modern urbanite: the land. It is the land of Taiwan that represents home and hearth, and thus the focus of any cultural shift within the ROC military should be one that focuses on the military's purpose of defending this land. Therefore this topic is mentioned first as it is a motif that must inform all future decisions on projects and policies as the military moves further into the twenty-first century. This would alleviate some of the ideological gap that exists between the traditional military culture and the realities of the people of Taiwan, in that the former is rooted in the Chinese identity, and of the ROC military being *in* Taiwan, but not *of* Taiwan. For decades now the goal of retaking the mainland has been abandoned, and yet the identity associated with that link has persisted. Instead, a new identity must be adopted, and that identity must focus on the land of Taiwan.

Conscription: First and foremost, plans to transition the ROC military to an All-Volunteer Force should be abandoned. For the reasons enumerated earlier in this chapter, the situation in Taiwan does not parallel even distantly the conditions in the United States when that country underwent its own AVF transition. The persistent threat of annexation by China makes this an unrealistic, as well as a potentially dangerous, goal. Not only is there insufficient budget to make a military paycheck competitive with what a young graduate can make in the civilian sector — meaning that manpower goals will never be met — but ending conscription would shift the military experience away from the majority of society, making the military a much less vital institution in Taiwan — it would place the armed forces on the fringes of society, and outside of the everyday experience of Taiwan's people. The opposite is needed.

Conscription is important in keeping up manpower numbers. But it is important for other reasons as well, if properly utilized. Conscripts properly trained not only in military discipline and the duties of a soldier, but also in how to mount guerilla campaigns, would in a matter of years create a large potential force of reservists with the knowledge and skills to mount a counteroffensive in the event of a PLA occupation of the island. Reservists are an integral component of a properly equipped and ready military force, and the ROC military currently has in excess of 140,000 reservists on the books, though they are being less than optimally leveraged. Currently, reservists must undergo training and administrative duties that amount to less than a week within a two-year period — far too short a time to ensure training and skills are up-to-date. Moreover, a reported 21 percent of reservists avoided even that minimal commitment in 2016, using loopholes in the rules (McCauley, 2016, p. 6). The time commitment demanded of reservists must be increased significantly, and their training be kept up to date to ensure a ready force can be called out in the event of a conflict, and moreover to ensure the necessary skills exist among a vast proportion of the country's males to form a resistance in the event of a Chinese occupation of Taiwan. A model from which ROC planners may draw inspiration is the example of Switzerland, whose rigorous and demanding mandatory military training, and follow-up reserve requirements, for all males is well known as the backbone of the nation's defense strategy.

In addition to making the country better prepared for an attack, conscription is a socialization mechanism whereby Taiwanese from all walks of life will live, eat, and train together to work as an effective unit. Soldiers serving their mandated service time, which should be expanded to between 12 and 18 months in order to provide an effective amount of training and experience, will come into contact with peers from all strata of Taiwan society. Taiwan has been called a multicultural society, and properly utilized, conscription would see Hakka, Hoklo, indigenous people, Benshengren, and Waishengren, all training together, helping to form a greater social unity for the nation. These friendships, moreover, carry over into post-military life, and have a great impact in fostering a more tolerant and unified society. Much has been written on the experience of Singapore: an ethnically diverse city-state where conscription has been credited with contributing to the building of a cohesive nation (Nair, 1995, p. 93). This example, more than the American one, is worthy of emulation. At the very least, more research is urged on how the Singapore example might be harnessed in a Taiwan context.

Training: Any effort to define the identity of an institution begins with education and training. The values espoused in military training courses must be those that are in line with the values of Taiwan's society today, not 40 years ago. It must be made clear to the soldiers serving in uniform that they are the primary line of defense protecting the values that they themselves hold to be of importance: democracy, liberty, the freedom to choose one's own path – just as the people of a nation must be free to choose a path for their nation. Continued focus on abstract and anachronistic concepts does little to make the military identity relevant in today's world.

Moreover, in terms of practical training, conscripts must feel that there is value in the work they are doing while in uniform. A common complaint among conscripts is that they spend their days performing menial tasks such as sweeping and yard work that have nothing to do with defending the nation (Lin, 2015). The current short service time and other training inefficiencies inevitably result in accidents that are both deadly and internationally embarrassing, not to mention having the potential to inadvertently trigger a shooting war given the state of tensions in the Taiwan Strait. One example is the admission by the ROC military on July 1, 2016 that a Navy NCO had accidentally fired a live supersonic Hsiung-feng II anti-ship missile from a corvette at Zuoying Navy Base, killing the captain of a fishing trawler near Penghu and stirring a diplomatic – though fortunately not military – backlash from China. More recently, on August 16, 2016, three ROC soldiers died when a CM-11 armored vehicle was driven off a three-meter-high bridge into Wangsha Stream in Pingtung county. A preliminary investigation cited a track jam as the cause of the accident, but more thorough training on how to deal with such unexpected occurrences would doubtless have saved lives.

If conscripts are engaged to serve for a period of 12 to 18 months, then this short time must be used effectively to provide the kind of training required not only of standing soldiers, but of reservists and of potential leaders. If the western experience in the Middle East has taught military planners any lessons, it is that Special Forces operators are the future. While it is unrealistic to expect every rank-and-file serviceman to develop SpecOps skills during their conscription period, training in the aforementioned guerilla techniques would be a good first step. Given the geopolitical realities in the Taiwan Strait, the only reason to oppose such a project would be the fear that such techniques could be turned against the home government. While this may have been a concern during the days of the Chiang regime, when the Taiwanese population was regarded as a potential threat, this no longer represents reality in today's Taiwan.

The training must be enjoyable, but it must be tasking, both physically and mentally. These concepts are not mutually exclusive: indeed, the only way to develop a sense of camaraderie among soldiers (which is the first step to developing positive morale) is to provide the opportunity for shared achievement. All too often, however, conscripts are parked in make-work jobs as they wait out their time until they can leave the military. Too often, soldiers are regarded by their managers as a cheap source of labor, rather than fighting men and women deserving of respect. At the time of writing, the conscription period has in some cases been reduced to a mere four months. Moreover, since the Hung Chung-chiu scandal, the military has – in good faith, it must be mentioned – stationed ambulances and medical aid personnel nearby training areas where conscripts do pushups, run laps, and perform other physical training activities. These efforts, while serving as a band-aid (both in real terms as well as public perception is concerned) against future occurrences of the unfortunate incident, serve only to highlight to conscripts that they are not being challenged, and that their efforts are not yielding any personal or group victories. Moreover, the short conscription period translates into a tacit acknowledgment by military leaders that conscription itself is a waste of time, and the reduced level of physical demands on the recruits come across as treating them like delicate, fragile things, not as warriors. This is not the way to create the opportunity for accomplishment, camaraderie, and pride.

Civilian Employees: The cynical use of conscripts for manual labor during their short conscription time means that the use of civilian employees must, therefore, be increased. They can be hired to perform the menial tasks now demoralizing soldiers so that conscripts can be freed up to focus on training. As already stated, there is too much of a tendency in the ROC military to view the issue of civilian–military interoperability as one which takes place at exclusively the upper echelons – the ministerial level, and among flag positions. What is equally important as the number of civilian PhDs that are hired are the number of menial jobs contracted out to free up soldiers' time for training. Moreover, the mindset that regards soldiers as cheap labor must be changed.

In addition to menial and managerial posts, civilian employees must also be hired for technical positions as well. The nature of modern warfare necessitates expertise with complex electronic systems, training to become proficient with which many conscripts do not have the time. Thus, until the military becomes an attractive career path for technically proficient job seekers, many technician and technologist jobs will best be performed by civilian contractors.

Transparency: It goes without saying that many aspects of military operations are security-sensitive and must be shielded from prying eyes, but incidents such as trainee deaths, which occur all too frequently, must not be covered up as this only compounds the negative perception when they are inevitably discovered. Such transparency must extend to the media, and can help to forge a new, better relationship with the nation's media outlets. For their part, the media too must stop using military scandals as sources for sensationalistic reporting, to focus instead on the facts and the social implication of such events.

One possible route to achieving this could be by expanding the use of embedded journalists in military units. The ROC military has proven itself very adept at reducing transparency and improving public relations through such methods as making bases and facilities open to the public on certain days, and on inviting the media to witness training exercises such as the annual Han Kuang Exercise. But in order to demystify the organization and create a better relationship with the public, it is equally important that the media and the public see the everyday lives of ordinary soldiers, airmen, and sailors, not just during high-profile drills. How do they live? Where do they sleep? What are their duties? The daily life of servicemen is extremely interesting to members of the public, as evidenced by numerous documentaries made all around the world, such as the BBC's "Sailor" about daily life on the aircraft carrier HMS *Ark Royal*, and the American equivalent, "Carrier," a 10-part series filmed aboard the USS *Nimitz*. Both documentaries share many commonalities, the most important of which is their frankness: they depict the excitement of a life in the military, but they also depict the boredom, the interpersonal conflicts, and they are not afraid to show sailors making mistakes and being punished by their superiors. Another excellent example is the 2010 documentary "Every Singaporean Son," which follows 15 young men from different backgrounds as they endure basic training, and in doing so experience a rite of passage that contributes to cementing their identity as Singaporean. Providing free access to TV crews and film-makers would go a long way to bringing the ROC military and the public closer together, and reducing the often adversarial nature of military—media interactions.

Cadets Youth Program: Another project that could be implemented in Taiwan is the institution of a youth league, which in structure would not be too dissimilar from the China Youth Corps, though without that organization's anti-Communist and colonial-era connotations. Rather, Taiwan could adopt a system similar to the one employed in Canada, whose Royal Canadian Sea Cadets, Air Cadets, and Army Cadets offer the opportunity for adolescents from around the country to work with their peers in learning environment-specific military skills and activities that benefit both the participants as well as the military itself. Sea Cadets, for example, learn about navigation, seamanship, sailing, and ropework, and they have opportunities to compete in regattas around the world against teams from other countries. Air Cadets, meanwhile, learn the skills of junior airmen and have the opportunity to fly training drones and even gliders, while Army Cadets learn orienteering, living off the land, first-aid, wilderness survival, target shooting, and other soldierly skills, all while still in high school. Most importantly, these groups focus on fun, sportsmanship, and building self-esteem and teamwork, with only a touch of military discipline. Not only would such a program be a boon to recruiting young people into lifelong military careers, but it would be indispensible as a means of fostering a healthier relationship between the military and society in general. Moreover, instructors in the cadets system, as well as former cadets themselves, represent the future leaders of the Taiwan military, and would bring with them a healthier respect for the military institution and its positive role in society — a far cry from the conscripts of today who count their daily mantou (bread ration) until they are finally released from service. In addition to being of benefit to the military, and to the country (as surely international connections would be made through the aforementioned regattas and other friendly competitions), such an organization would be beneficial to the young people themselves, who are at an age when they seek to belong in a group outside of family, and thus are often attracted to joining gangs and other dangerous pursuits. This organization would offer a positive alternative.

Ethnic Indigenous Regiments: For countless generations, the indigenous ethnic groups of Taiwan have had to contend with various colonizers who sought to assimilate them and force them to give up their customs, beliefs, and traditional lifestyles in order to adopt the identity of the majority. This represents a lost opportunity for the Taiwan military, which should instead authorize the formation and training of indigenous regiments that would not only benefit from training in modern military tactics, but employ the traditional skills of indigenous heritage, such as hunting, tracking, and living off the land. This comes back to the previous notes on refocusing the ethic of the military to one that focuses on the land, and there are arguably no peoples in Taiwan who know the land better than the nation's indigenous groups. While such regiments would greatly benefit the military in general, as those skills are shared and as the public comes to view the military as an organization that respects the diversity of Taiwan's peoples, it would also benefit the indigenous groups themselves, many of whose traditions and skills are in danger of disappearing for lack of opportunity to pass them on. The creation of indigenous units and regiments would go a long way toward recognizing the value in those traditional skills, and helping the peoples themselves to rebuild their links with their heritage.

It should be noted that such regiments are not unprecedented, with Cherokee and Choctaw battalions in the United States, and such famously fierce units as the Gurkhas making up regiments in the British Army. In Taiwan, indigenous native soldiers led by indigenous officers could be organized according to indigenous groups, or across them. Highly trained and accomplished NCOs of such units could furthermore be tasked to teach skills such as tracking, primitive hunting, wilderness survival, and escape-and-evasion techniques to regular army platoons as well. This would not only serve as a transmission of invaluable skills and knowledge, but help foster a greater understanding and respect for the nation's indigenous people among the Han Chinese majority. As has been observed earlier in this text, one of the training objectives of the Taiwan military should be to imbue its soldiers, and especially reservists, with guerilla fighting skills and tactics, and methods of fighting asymmetrically, should Chinese troops occupy the island. There would be no better teacher of such skills and such knowledge than the peoples whose ancestors have lived on this land for thousands of years. Moreover, this would go a long way toward dispelling the myth that the military remains the KMT army.

12.4. CONCLUSION

A military does not run on weapons, equipment, and manpower numbers. A military runs on *esprit de corps*, honor, and morale. History has shown, time and again, that even a numerically inferior, less-equipped force has the potential to emerge victorious against a larger foe if these intangible elements are present. The current state of the ROC armed forces is often characterized as being in dire need of reform, with analysts and journalists citing a plethora of problems including inadequate training, low morale, poor discipline, limited resources, and a lack of strategic guidance among officers (McCauley, 2016, p. 5). The ROC military is in a doldrums – as evidenced by the current research, the public has little confidence or trust in their military, while remaining acutely aware of the need for it. Even President Tsai Ing-wen has stated that Taiwan's military is in need of "drastic" reforms, and while there has been much analysis as to what strategic and weapons systems should be adopted by ROC defense planners, relatively little is being written on how to create a more relevant military within the current state of Taiwan society. This research is aimed at that endeavor: not to be the final word on the topic, but rather to spark a discussion of the issue – a discussion that is sorely needed, and yet is not taking place. The recommendations enumerated above are but aspects of that discussion: many analysts, sociologists, politicians, and other interested parties will no doubt have differing opinions on the relative value of such suggestions, but at least then they will be having this much-needed discussion. According to Richard Beckhard, a pioneer in the field of organization development, organizational change can be successful when certain conditions are met. He illustrates the phenomenon using the Change Formula and the model of Beckhard and Harris (1987):

$$D \times V \times F > R$$

wherein D represents dissatisfaction with the current state of affairs; V represents a shared vision of a more amenable future state; and F represents first steps taken on a roadmap for achieving the shared vision, the product of which are greater than the R, or resistance to change, within the organization needing change. In the Taiwan context, the

D — dissatisfaction — is evident. Virtually all quarters, from the government to the populace, to the serving military members themselves, are dissatisfied with the current state of affairs. The problem arises when one seeks to find V — a shared vision of a more amenable future state. Because of the unique cultural, social, and political divide in Taiwan, finding a shared vision of the future remains a daunting task. The current volume seeks to illuminate some of the intricacies of that lack of unity, by measuring the dependent variables related to military perception against the independent variables of self-identification. Quantitative research of this nature is imperative to move beyond mere public opinion surveys in order to define the differences and hence find areas of convergence and therefore shared vision. It is the opinion of this researcher that a good start for this shared vision is the land: Despite all the differences in belief and opinion among the various groups in Taiwan, it is the land that represents home, family, and the most likely potential source of unity and shared vision, especially as regards the defense of the nation, or rather, the defense of the land. Once such a shared vision is articulated, then policy can be made in the task of reforming the military and its place in society: only then can F — first steps — be taken on a road-map to achieve this vision. Until then, the reverse of the Beckhard formula will remain true, and R — resistance to change — will continue to outweigh efforts to effect change.

In terms of dissatisfaction: pollsters have illustrated it, and ordinary citizens seem to instinctively be aware of it, but so far few attempts have been made to measure it using a theoretical framework such as is done in the current volume using the PMMM. Designed as a means to conceptualize the evolution of militaries from the modern to the postmodern eras, the PMMM is an excellent analytical tool for understanding the current state of the ROC military/society relationship. Research such as this will become an indispensable tool to be used by government and military planners seeking to fix the problems that exist today. Thus far, without a comprehensive and science-based understanding of the problems besetting the ROC military, the attempts at remedy have largely been band-aid solutions, which risk exacerbating the problems in the long term. Rather, a well-researched, carefully constructed plan is needed to transform the ROC military, not merely from conscription-based to an AVF, but from an institution distrusted by the society it protects, to one that is a source of national pride. Such a transformation will remain an impossibility without the understanding provided by the sort of sociological research for which this project represents both a humble beginning and a clarion call.

REFERENCES

Alagappa, M. (2001). *Coercion and Governance: The Declining Political Role of the Military in Asia*. Stanford, CA: Stanford UP.

Arrigo, L. G. (1980). The Industrial Workforce of Young Women in Taiwan. *Critical Asian Studies*, *12*(2), 25–30.

Arrington, A. (2002). Cautious Reconciliation: The Change in Societal–Military Relations in Germany and Japan Since the End of the Cold War. *Armed Forces & Society*, *28*(4), 531–554.

Au, C.-t. (2008). *Modernist Aesthetics in Taiwanese Poetry Since the 1950s*. Leiden: Brill.

Axelbank, A. (1963). Chiang Kai-shek's Silent Enemies. *The Harper's Monthly*, 46–53.

Banning-Lover, R., & Clarke, J. S. (2016). Six Countries Making Progress on LGBT Rights. *The Guardian*, February 10.

Beckhard, R., & Harris, R. T. (1987). *Organizational Transitions: Managing Complex Change*. Reading, MA: Addison-Wesley Pub.

Bell, D. A., & Jayasuriya, K. (1995). Understanding Illiberal Democracy: A Framework. In D. Bell, D. Brown,

K. Jayasuriya, & D. M. Jones (Ed.), *Towards Illiberal Democracy in Asia Pacific*. London: MacMillan.

Bickford, T. (2007). Searching for a Twenty-First Century Officer Corps. In D. M. Finkelstein & K. Gunness (Eds.), *Civil—Military Relations in Today's China: Swimming in a New Sea* (pp. 171–186). Armonk, NY: East Gate.

Blundell, D. (Ed.). (2012). *Taiwan Since Martial Law: Society, Culture, Politics, Economics*. Berkeley, CA: University of California, & Taipei: National Taiwan University Press.

Bornman, E. (1999). Self-Image and Ethnic Identification in South Africa. *The Journal of Social Psychology*, *139*(4), 411–425.

Bowers, F. The Hakujin Experience. Japanese American Veterans Association. Retrieved from http://www.javadc.org/prelude.htm

Brooks, C. (2014). When it Comes to Women in Management, U.S. Doesn't Lead. *Business News Daily*, March 11.

Buchanan, N. T., Settles, I. H., Hall, A. T., & O'Connor, R. C. (2014). A Review of Organizational Strategies for Reducing Sexual Harassment: Insights from the US Military. *Journal of Social Issues*, *70*(4), 687–702.

Bullard, M. R. (1997). *The Soldier and the Citizen: The Role of the Military in Taiwan's Development*. Armonk, NY: M.E. Sharpe.

Castro, C. A., Kintzle, S., Schuyler, A. C., Lucas, C. L., & Warner, C. H. (2015). Sexual Assault in the Military. *Current Psychiatry Reports*, *17*(7), 54.

Chang, C. C.-h., & Tien, H.-m. (1996). *Taiwan's Electoral Politics and Democratic Transition: Riding the Third Wave.* Armonk, NY: M.E. Sharpe.

Chang, Y. H. (1994). Household Compositions and the Attitude of Support for Parents in a Changing Society: The Case of Taiwan. *National Taiwan University Journal of Sociology, 23*, 1–34.

Chase, M. S. (2006). Defense Reform and Civilian Control in Taiwan. *China Brief, 6*, 22.

Chen, C.-s. (2009a). *Taiwan and the Development of a Late-Modern Military.* Dissertation, State University of New York.

Chen, M.-H. (1999). *The Relationship of Mothers and Daughters-In-Law in Urban Chinese Families.* Dissertation, Texas Woman's University.

Chen, Y. W. (2009b). The Evolution of Taiwan's Military Strategy: Convergence and Dissonance. *China Brief, IX*(23), 8–12.

Cheng, W.-Y., & Liao, L.-L. (1993). Women Managers in Taiwan. *International Studies of Management & Organization, 23*(4), 65–86.

Christensen, T. J. (1996). *Useful Adversaries: Grand Strategy, Domestic Mobilization, and Sino-American Conflict, 1947-1958.* Princeton, NJ: Princeton UP.

Chu, Y.-H. (2004). Taiwan's National Identity Politics and the Prospect of Cross-Strait Relations. *Asian Survey, 44*(4), 484–512.

Cohen, A. (1969). Political Anthropology: The Analysis of the Symbolism of Power Relations. *Man, 4*(2), 215–235.

Costa, R. P., & Ivenicki, A. (2016). Multiculturalism and Peace Studies for Education Provision in Time of Diverse Democracies. BCES Conference Books. *Proceedings. of XIV BCES Conference 2016—Education Provision to Everyone: Comparing Perspectives from Around the World*, Bulgaria: Investpress. 226–232.

DeBary, W. T. (1969). *The Buddhist Tradition in India, China and Japan*. New York, NY: Vintage.

Dyvik, S. L. (2013). Women as 'practitioners' and 'targets'. *International Feminist Journal of Politics*, 16(3), 410–429.

Edmonds, M., & Tsai, M. M. (2006). *Taiwan's Defense Reform*. London: Routledge.

Feinman, I. R. (2000). *Citizenship Rites: Feminist Soldiers and Feminist Antimilitarists*. New York, NY: New York University Press.

Freedman, R., Thornton, A., & Yang, L.-s. (1994). Determinants of Co-Residence in Extended Households. In A. Thornton & H.-S. Lin (Ed.), *Social Change and the Family in Taiwan* (pp. 335–358). Chicago, IL: University of Chicago.

Funabashi, Y.. (2002). The New Roles of the Military in the 21st Century: The Japanese Perspective. *Proceedings, International Symposium on Security Affairs, The National Institute for Defense Studies*, Tokyo.

Geertz, C. (1973). *The Interpretation of Cultures: Selected Essays*. New York, NY: Basic.

Gold, M. (2013). Taiwan a Testing Ground for Chinese Cyber Army. *Technology News*, July 18.

Gold, T. B. (1996). Taiwan Society at the Fin De Siécle. *The China Quarterly*, 148, 1091–1114.

Goldbach, J. T., & Castro, C. A. (2016). Lesbian, Gay, Bisexual, and Transgender (LGBT) Service Members: Life After Don't Ask, Don't Tell. *Current Psychiatry Reports*, *18*(6), 56.

Guy, N. (2005). *Peking Opera and Politics in Taiwan*. Urbana, IL: University of Illinois.

"H.R. 2479 – 96th Congress: Taiwan Relations Act." www. GovTrack.us. 1979. April 26, 2018. Retrieved from https:// www.govtrack.us/congress/bills/96/hr2479

Harrell, S., & Huang, J. (1994). Introduction: Change and Contention in Taiwan's Cultural Scene. In S. Harrell & J. Huang (Ed.), *Cultural Change in Postwar Taiwan*. (pp. 1–18). Boulder, CO: Westview.

Harrison, M. (2016). *Legitimacy, Meaning and Knowledge in the Making of Taiwanese Identity*. Springer.

Hempel, L. (2004). What's it worth to you? The questionable value of instrumentalist approaches to ethnic identification. *International Journal of Comparative Sociology*, *45*(3–4), 253–275.

Hochschild, A. R., & Machung, A. (1989). *The Second Shift: Working Parents and the Revolution at Home*. New York, NY: Viking.

Hsiao, H.-H. M. (Ed.) (2014). *Chinese Middle Classes: Taiwan, Hong Kong, Macao, and China*. London: Taylor & Francis Group.

Hsiau, A. C. (2000). Contemporary Taiwanese Cultural Nationalism (Routledge Studies in the Modern History of Asia) (1st ed.). New York, NY: Routledge.

Hsu, F. L. K. (1971). A Hypothesis on Kinship and Culture. In F. L. K. Hsu (Ed.), *Kinship and culture*. Chicago, IL: Aldine.

Hu, M.-W. (2003). Many Small Antelopes Make a Dragon. *Futures*, *35*(4), 379–392.

Hunter-Chester, D. (2016). *Creating Japan's Ground Self-Defense Force, 1945-2015: A Sword Well Made*. Lanham, MD: Lexington Books.

Isajiw, W.. (1992, April 2). Definition and Dimensions of Ethnicity: A Theoretical Framework. Joint Canada-United States Conference on the Measurement of Ethnicity. Ontario, Canada, Ottawa.

Jacobs, A. (2014). For Asia's Gays, Taiwan Stands Out as Beacon. *New York Times*, October 29.

Janowitz, M. (1960). *The Professional Soldier, a Social and Political Portrait*. Glencoe, IL: Free Press.

Kamarck, K. N. (2016). *Women in Combat: Issues for Congress*. Congressional Research Service Washington United States.

Kastner, J. (2011). Military Scandals Test Taiwan. *Asia Times Online*, March 18.

Kim, K. (2009). Post-Cold War Civil–Military Relations in South Korea: Toward a Postmodern Military? Retrieved from https://ubir.buffalo.edu/xmlui/handle/10477/45399

King, A. C. (2015). Women Warriors: Female Accession to Ground Combat. *Armed Forces & Society*, *41*(2), 379–387.

Kurashina, Y. (2003). Military Sociology in Japan. In J. Callaghan & F. Kernic (Eds.), *Armed Forces and*

International Security: Global Trends and Issues (pp. 151–155). Munster: Lit Verlag.

Laurence, J. H., & Matthews, M. D. (2012). *The Oxford Handbook of Military Psychology*. New York, NY: Oxford UP.

Lin, S. (2015April 13). Netizen's List of Military Hates Strikes Chord. *The Taipei Times,* April 13.

Liou, L.-y. (2006). Queer Theory and Politics in Taiwan: The Cultural Translation and (Re)Production of Queerness in and Beyond Taiwan Lesbian/Gay/Queer Activism. *NTU Studies in Language & Literature*, *14*, 123–154.

Lomsky-Feder, E., & Sasson-Levy, O. (2016). The Effects of Military Service on Women's Lives from the Narrative Perspective. In H. Carreiras, C. Castro, & S. Frederic (Eds.), *Researching the Military* (pp. 94–107). New York, NY: Routledge.

Lu, H.-f. (2000). *Family Types and Marital Power: A Field Study in Taiwan*. Dissertation, Harvard University.

Marsh, R. M. (1998). Gender and Pay in Taiwan: Men's Attitudes in 1963 and 1991. *International Journal of Comparative Sociology*, *39*(1), 115–137.

McCauley, K. (2016). Taiwan's Military Reforms and Strategy: Reset Required. *China Brief*, *16*(13), 5–9.

McGlynn, A. D. A. M., & Monforti, J. L. (2016, October). nd "The Poverty Draft? Exploring the Role of Socioeconomic Status in US Military Recruitment of Hispanic Students". In Annual Meeting of American Political Science Association, Washington, DC.[Online]. Retrieved from http://ssrn.com/abstract (Vol. 1643790, No. 8).

McGuire, A. (2017). *Sex Scandal: The Drive to Abolish Male and Female*. Washington, DC: Regnery Publishing.

Ministry of Defense, Taiwan. (1996). *Republic of China, 1996 National Defense Report*. Taipei: Li Ming.

Moskos, C. C., Williams, J. A., & Segal, D. R. (2000). *The Postmodern Military: Armed Forces After the Cold War*. New York, NY: Oxford UP.

Muyard, F. (2012). Taiwanese National Identity, Cross-Strait Economic Interaction, and the Integration Paradigm. In P. C. Y. Chow (Ed.), *National Identity and Economic Interest: Taiwan's Competing Options and Their Implications for Regional Stability* (pp. 153–186). New York, NY: Palgrave Macmillan US.

"National Population and Housing Census". (2014). Directorate General of Budget, Accounting and Statistics. Executive Yuan.

Nair, E. (1995). Conscription and Nation-Building in Singapore: A Psychological Analysis. *Journal of Human Values*, *1*(1), 93–102.

Palm Center. (2002). Asia's Silence on Gays in Military Broken by Taiwan. *Palm Center*, May 15.

Rankin, M. B. (1975). The Emergence of Women at the End of Ching: The Case of Ch'u Chin. In M. Wolf & R. Witcke (Ed.), *Women in Chinese Society* (pp. 39–66). Stanford: Stanford UP.

Robinson, P. (2016). *When Soldiers Say No: Selective Conscientious Objection in the Modern Military*. London: Taylor & Francis Group.

Rosen, L. N. (2003). Cohesion and the Culture of Hypermasculinity in U.S. Army Units. *Armed Forces & Society, 29*(3), 325–351.

Ross, M. H. (2009). Culture in Comparative Political Analysis. In M. I. Lichbach & A. S. Zuckerman (Ed.), *Comparative Politics Rationality, Culture, and Structure* (pp. 134–161). Cambridge: Cambridge University Press.

Roy, D. (2003). *Taiwan: A Political History*. Ithaca, NY: Cornell University Press.

Rubinstein, M. A. (2013). The Evolution of Taiwan's Economic Miracle 1945-2000: Personal Accounts and Political Narratives. In F. B. Douglas & M. A. Rubinstein (Ed.), *Technology Transfer Between the US, China and Taiwan* (pp. 36–58). Abingdon Oxfordshire: Routledge.

Selznick, P.. (1960). *The Organizational Weapon; A Study of Bolshevik Strategy and Tactics*. Glencoe, IL: Free Press.

Setzekorn, E. (2014). Military Reform in Taiwan: The Lafayette Scandal, National Defense Law and All-Volunteer Force. *American Journal of Chinese Studies, 21*(1), 7–19.

Shepherd, L. J. (2008). *Gender, Violence and Security: Discourse as Practice*. London: Zed.

Singer, P. W. (2007). *Corporate Warriors: The Rise of the Privatized Military Industry*. Ithaca, NY: Cornell University Press.

Smith, N. (2011, December 7). Contemporary Issues Facing Women in the Military. Web log post. Article Myriad.

Speare, A., Liu, K., & Tsay, C.-l. (1988). *Urbanization and Development: The Rural–Urban Transition in Taiwan*. Boulder, CO: Westview Press.

Stachowitsch, S. (2012). Military Gender Integration and Foreign Policy in the United States: A Feminist International Relations Perspective. *Security Dialogue*, *43*(4), 305–321.

Stewart, J. M. F. J. B. (2017). Trends in Gender and Racial Equity in Retention and Promotion of Officers. *Managing Diversity in the Military: Research Perspectives from the Defense Equal Opportunity Management Institute*. New York, NY: Routledge.

Street, A. E., Stafford, J., Mahan, C. M., & Hendricks, A. (2008). Sexual Harassment and Assault Experienced by Reservists During Military Service: Prevalence and Health Correlates. *The Journal of Rehabilitation Research and Development*, *45*(3), 409–420.

Su, C. (2009). *Taiwan's Relations with Mainland China: A Tail Wagging Two Dogs*. London: Routledge.

Swaine, M. D., & Mulvenon, J. C. (2001). *Taiwan's Foreign and Defense Policies: Features and Determinants*. Santa Monica, CA: Rand Corporation.

"Taiwanese Women Embrace 'Male' Careers but Gender Gap Remains". (2013). *South China Morning Post*, November 24.

Tai, H.-c. (1974). *Land Reform and Politics: A Comparative Analysis*. Berkeley, CA: University of California.

Taiwan National Security and Defense Law and Regulations Handbook. (2007). Intl Business Pubns USA.

Taiwan Today. (2016). Female Breadwinner Numbers Hit Record High in Taiwan. Taiwan Today. September 19.

Tajfel, H. (1979). An Integrative Theory of Intergroup Conflict. In J. C. Turner (Ed.), *The Social Psychology of*

Intergroup Relations (pp. 33—48). Pacific Grove, CA: Brooks/Cole.

Templeman, K. A., Uzonyi, G. J., & Flores, T. E. (2015). Threats, Alliances, and Electorates: Why Taiwan's Defense Spending has Declined as China's Has Risen. Working paper. CCDRL, Stanford University.

Tsai, Y.-m., & Yi, C.-c. (1987). Persistence and Change of the Chinese Family Values: The Taiwanese Case. In R.-s. Yang & H.-y. Chiu (Ed.), *Taiwanese Society in Transition* (20th ed., Vol. B), Taipei: Institute of Ethnology, Academia Sinica. Monograph Ser.

Tsai, Y. Y. (2014). Genetic Science and Identity Politics: Indigenous DNA, the Origin of the Taiwanese, and the Emergence of Bio-Multiculturalism. *Taiwan She Hui Xue*, *28*, 1.

Tuan, Y.-f. (1982). *Segmented Worlds and Self: Group Life and Individual Consciousness*. Minneapolis, MN: University of Minnesota.

Tucker, N. B. (2005). *Dangerous Strait: The U.S.-Taiwan-China Crisis*. New York, NY: Columbia University Press.

Tung, M.-C., Huang, J.-Y., Keh, H.-C., & Wai, S.-S. (2009). The Initiative of Distance E-Training System for Advanced Military Education in Taiwan. *Tamkang Journal of Science and Engineering*, *12*(4), 489—498.

Turner, J. (1982). Towards a Cognitive Redefinition of the Social Group. In H. Tajfel (Ed.), *Social Identity and Intergroup Relations* (pp. 15—40). Cambridge: Cambridge University Press.

Turton, M. A. (2016, June 12). Re: The Diplomat on the Evolution of the New Taiwan Identity: Plus Ca Change. Web log comment. The View from Taiwan.

Turton, M. A. (2016b, May 24). Ma Ying-jeou's Legendary (Trade) Millions. The Diplomat.

Wang, T. Y., & Liu, I.-C. (2004). Contending Identities in Taiwan: Implications for Cross-Strait Relations. *Asian Survey*, *44*(4), 568–590.

Whaley, A. L. (2005). Racial Self-Designation and Disorder in African American Psychiatric Patients. *Journal of Black Psychology*, *31*(1), 87–104.

Williams, T. K., & Thornton, M. C. (1998). Social Construction of Ethnicity Versus Personal Experience: The Case of Afro-Amerasians. *Journal of Comparative Family Studies Comparative Perspectives On Black Family Life*, *29*(2), 255–267.

Woo-Cumings, M. J.-E. (1998). National Security and the Rise of the Developmental State in South Korea and Taiwan. In H. S. Rowen (Ed.), *Behind East Asian Growth: The Political and Social Foundations of Prosperity* (pp. 319–337). London: Routledge.

Wu, E. Y. (2017). Taiwan's Failure to Face the Threat from China. *The New York Times*. May 18.

Wu, R.-h. (2008, July 31). Bio-Politicizing Ethnicity – a Preliminary Observation on Taiwan's Ethnic Relations and the Transforming National Identity. American Sociological Association Annual Meeting. Sheraton Boston and the Boston Marriott Copley Place, Boston.

Yi, C.-c., & Chang, Y.-h. (1995). Change of family structure and marital power in Taiwan. In N. Chen Y.-l. Liu, & M.-O.

Hsieh (Ed.), *Families, human resources and social development*. Taipei: Graduate Institute of Sociology, National Chengchi University.

Yi, C.-c., & Lu, Y.-h. (1996). A Review on Family and Women Studies in Taiwan. In H. H. Hsiao & Y. H. Chang (Ed.), *The Development and Exchange of Sociology in Taiwan, Hong Kong and China*. Taipei: Taiwanese Sociological Association.

Yu, W.-h. (2015). *Women and Employment in Taiwan. Taiwan-U.S. Quarterly Analysis No. 19 of 20*. Brookings Institution.

Yu, W.-H., & Su, K.-H. (2006). Gender, Sibship Structure, and Educational Inequality in Taiwan: Son Preference Revisited. *Journal of Marriage and Family*, *68*(4), 1057–1068.

INDEX

Age-old military ritual, 132
Agricultural assistance program, 140
Air Cadets, 175
"All-out defense", 89
All-Volunteer Force (AVF), 18, 47, 169
  military, 132
  transition, 162–167
Alternative service system, 78
Anti-communism, 88, 138, 146
Armed Forces of Republic of China (ROC). *See* ROC Armed Forces
Army Cadets, 175
"Asian values" concepts, 133
Association of Promotion of Human Rights in Military (APHRM), 140
Atomic weapons, 16

British Special Air Service (SAS), 30

Cadets youth program, 175–176
Canadian Women's Royal Canadian Naval Service (Wrens), 31
CCP, 56, 58, 91
China
  military in, 156–159
  see also ROC armed forces
  threat, 52–53
China Television Company (CTV), 146
Chinese Civil War, 52
Chinese Communist Party, 55
Chinese culture, women role in, 114–117
Chinese Television System (CTS), 95, 138
CIA, 24
Civilian contractors, 100
Civilian employees, 28–30, 99–102, 101, 173
Civilian job market, 100
Cold War, 15, 17, 18
Combat leaders, 94

Communism, 3, 23, 26, 88
Confucian filial piety,
     106–107
Confucian ideal, 115
Confucian structure of
     society, 115
Conscientious objection
     (CO), 38–40, 75
   in ROC military, 75–81
Conscription, 68–69,
     169–170
Cosmopolitan army, 157
Council of Labor Affairs
     (1999), 122
Cultural Revolution, 137
Culturalist perspective,
     47–49
Culture war, 54, 56–58

Democratization era, 45
Demographics, 164–165
Dominant military
     professional, 20–21,
     96
   dimension, 154
   public perception, 98–99
   in ROC military, 93–98
DPP, 46, 97–98

Epiphenomenon approach,
     43
Ethnic cleavages, 139
Ethnic conflicts, 17
Ethnic indigenous
     regiments, 176–177
Ethnic self-identification
   culturalist perspective,
     47–49

identity issue in Taiwan,
     44–47
"Every Singaporean Son"
     documentary (2010),
     174–175

Familization, 48
Female integration, 33
Force Modification Plan, 71
Force structure, 18–19,
     67–69
   force structure in ROC,
     69–75
FuBing militia system, 68

Gates Commission Report,
     164
General Political Warfare
     Department, 146
Geopolitical scenario, 154
Great Leap Forward, 137

Han dynasty, 68
"Heaven's decree", 55
Homosexuality, 130
Homosexuals in ROC
     military, 36–38, 129
   research findings,
     133–134
Humanitarian Assistance
     and Disaster Relief
     (HA/DR), 20

Ideological polarization,
     148
"Innovative and
     asymmetrical
     warfare", 161

Instrumentalist approach, 43
Islamic fundamentalist forces, 113
Islamic terrorism, 19, 52

Japan Air Self-Defense Force, 156−157
Japan Ground Self-Defense Force, 156−157
Japan Maritime Self-Defense Force, 156−157
Japanese military units, 156−159
Japanese society, 157
Joint Commission on Rural Reconstruction (JCRR), 70

Korea, military in, 156−159
Kuomintang (KMT), 45−46, 52, 58, 136, 139, 147, 167
  rulers, 84−85
  troops, 136

Land, focus on, 168−169
Late modern (1945−1990) militaries, 18, 19, 25, 37, 39, 158
Law enforcement authorities, 131
Lone-wolf terrorists, 17

Major mission definition, 19−20
Marital status, indicator of, 105−106

Media relations, 25−27
  with ROC military, 145−150
Military
  community, 35−36
  feminist perspective of women's role in, 111−114
  homosexuals in, 36−38
  members' attitudes, 14
  military-dependent variables, 158
  military-first forces, 109
  mission, 87−88
  new military ethic, 167−177
  operations, 100
  public attitude toward, 21−24
  scandals, 174
  women's role in, 30−35
  see also Postmodern military model (PMMM)
Military operations other than war (MOOTW), 20, 140
Military Service System Act, 76−77
MND, 97, 138
Modern (pre-Cold War/ 1900−1945) military, 15, 18, 19, 25, 31, 39, 158
Morale problem, 161−162
Moskos's institutional vs. occupational (I/O) model, 35, 109

Multicultural society, 170
Mutually assured
    destruction (MAD), 16

National Defense
    Organization Act in
    (2002), 96
National Defense Report
    (2017), 161
National Policy
    Foundation, 120–121
National Revolutionary
    Army. *See* ROC
    Armed Forces
National unity, 138, 147
National Women's League,
    108
Natural disasters, 140
Navy NCO, 171
News media, 25
Non-commissioned officers
    (NCOs), 36
Nuclear weapons, 16

Offensive defense, 89
Officer-type contractors,
    100

People's Liberation Army
    (PLA), 53
People's Republic of China
    (PRC), 56–57
Policy recommendations
    AVF transition, 162–167
    morale problem,
        161–162
    new military ethic,
        167–177

Political imperative,
    163–164
Political Warfare Cadres
    Academy, 123
Political warfare
    department, 123–124
Population-centric
    counterinsurgency
    theory, 113
Post martial-law period,
    136
Post-9/11 conflicts, 112
Postmodern designation,
    135, 154
Postmodern era
    (1990–present), 18
Postmodern military model
    (PMMM), 11–13,
    20–21, 27, 47, 51, 60,
    64, 149, 151, 154,
    157–158
    civilian employees,
        28–30
    CO, 38–40
    dimensions, 14
    dominant military
        professional, 20–21
    force structure, 18–19
    homosexuals in military,
        36–38
    major mission definition,
        19–20
    media relations, 25–27
    perceived threat, 15–18
    public attitude toward
        military, 21–24
    spouses and military
        community, 35–36

women's role in military,
30–35
Postmodern soldier, 19
PR effort, 137
PR exercise, 138
Proscribed postmodern
military, 157
Public attitudes, 135
toward military, 21–24
toward ROC military,
135–145
Public perception
of dominant military
professional, 98–99
of mission, 90–91
of threat, 58–65

Regression, 133
Republic of China (ROC),
12–13, 47, 51, 53, 54
Republic of China Armed
Forces. See ROC
Armed Forces
Republic of Taiwan, 56
Reservists, 169–170
ROC armed forces, 1, 2, 5,
7–8, 18, 69, 71, 74,
84, 90, 95, 103, 151,
154, 161, 165, 168,
174
civilian employees in,
99–102
civilians in, 28–29
CO in, 75–81
conscription, 68–69
dominant military
professional in, 93–98
force structure in, 69–75

homosexuals in, 38, 129
media relations with,
145–150
military stance, 89
mission, 89
PMMM and, 60
public attitudes toward,
135–145
reorganization project, 72
research findings,
133–134
society–military
relationship, 90
women in, 112, 123–127
ROC military. See ROC
armed forces

Satellite Broadcasting Act,
148
Scandinavian model, 121
Search and rescue (SAR),
89
Second World War, 16
Self-defense era, 71
Sexual harassment, 33–34
Sino-American Mutual
Defense Treaty, 70
Situational approach, 43
Small-and medium-sized
enterprises (SMEs),
118
Social and cultural factors,
105
Social Identity Theory, 43
Society–military
relationship, 90
Sociological dependent
variables, 158

Soldier-type contractors, 100

South Korea's military, 158

South Korean military's assessment, 158

SpecOps skills, 172

Spouses and military community, 35–36, 103–110

"Strong defense and layered deterrence", 161

Subjective approach, 43

Sui dynasty, 68

Taipei Times, The, 162

Taiwan
  advanced military education system in, 95
  democratization, 100, 124
  family ideology in, 107
  identity issue in, 44–47
  military, 176
  population, 172
  society, 132, 144
  threat perception, 51–65
  women's movement in, 121–123

Taiwan Garrison Command, 71

"Taiwan Miracle", 117

Taiwan Relations Act (TRA), 71

Taiwan Strait Crisis, third, 89

Taiwan Television Enterprise (TTV), 146

Taiwanese identity, 41

Tang dynasty, 68

Tangwai opposition, 147

Taoist concept of complementary forces, 130

Terrorism, 6, 11, 17, 19, 52

"Threat of enemy invasion", 60

Threat perception, 6, 11, 16–18, 29, 67
  among Taiwanese "Mainlanders", 54–56
  culture war, 56–58
  public perception of threat, 58–65

Tiānmìng. *See* "Heaven's decree"

Transparency, 173–175

Tsai administration, 162

United States Military Academy, 124

Urban tertiary employment, 106

US army desire for change, 167

US Women's Army Corps (WAC), 31

Vietnam War, 27
  opposition to, 166–167

West Point. *See* United
  States Military
  Academy
White Terror, 84
Women and military
  feminist perspective of
    women's role,
    111–114
  movement in Taiwan,
    121–123

  in ROC military,
    123–127
  role, 30–35, 114–117
  in workforce, 117–121
Women's Auxiliary Air
  Force (WAAF), 31
Women's League, 109
World War I (WWI), 31
World War II (WWII),
  15–16